Winner of the L. E. Phillabaum Poetry Award for 2017

BLACKOUT STARLIGHT

NEW AND SELECTED POEMS
1997–2015

Bruce Bond

Louisiana State University Press  Baton Rouge

Published by Louisiana State University Press
Copyright © 2017 by Bruce Bond
All rights reserved
Manufactured in the United States of America
LSU Press Paperback Original
First printing

Designer: Michelle A. Neustrom
Typeface: Adagio Serif
Printer and binder: LSI

Poems herein have been selected from *Radiography* (Rochester, NY: BOA Editions, 1997), *The Throats of Narcissus* (Fayetteville: University of Arkansas Press, 2001), *Blind Rain* (Baton Rouge: LSU Press, 2008), *The Visible* (Baton Rouge: LSU Press, 2012), *For the Lost Cathedral* (Baton Rouge: LSU Press, 2015), and the following:

Cinder. Copyright © 2003 by Bruce Bond. Reprinted with the permission of Etruscan Press. www.etruscanpress.org

Peal. Copyright © 2009 by Bruce Bond. Reprinted with the permission of Etruscan Press. www.etruscanpress.org

Choir of the Wells. Copyright © 2013 by Bruce Bond. Reprinted with the permission of Etruscan Press. www.etruscanpress.org

The Other Sky. Copyright © 2015 by Bruce Bond. Reprinted with the permission of Etruscan Press. www.etruscanpress.org

Uncollected poems in this volume first appeared in *Blue Lyra, Poetry East,* and *Seattle Review.*

Library of Congress Cataloging-in-Publication Data

Names: Bond, Bruce, 1954– author.
Title: Blackout starlight : new and selected poems, 1997–2015 / Bruce Bond.
Description: Baton Rouge : Louisiana State University Press, [2017]
Identifiers: LCCN 2016027498| ISBN 978-0-8071-6533-1 (pbk. : alk. paper) | ISBN 978-0-8071-6534-8 (pdf) | ISBN 978-0-8071-6535-5 (epub) | ISBN 978-0-8071-6536-2 (mobi)
Classification: LCC PS3552.O5943 A6 2017 | DDC 811/.54—dc23
LC record available at https://lccn.loc.gov/2016027498

The paper in this book meets the guidelines for permanence and durability of the Committee on Production Guidelines for Book Longevity of the Council on Library Resources. ∞

For Nicki

CONTENTS

FROM *Radiography* (1997)

Native Tongue ∗ 3
Homage to Szymon Laks ∗ 4
Divorce ∗ 6
North: 1991 ∗ 7
The Possible ∗ 9
Confederate Dead ∗ 10
Pomegranate ∗ 12
Radiography ∗ 13

FROM *The Throats of Narcissus* (2001)

Cruor Dei ∗ 21
1979 ∗ 24
The Sirens of Los Angeles ∗ 26
Oval ∗ 28
Thelonious Sphere Monk ∗ 30
The Flies ∗ 32
The Throats of Narcissus ∗ 34

FROM *Cinder* (2003)

The Fall ∗ 41
Rope ∗ 45
The Island City of Dmitri Shostakovich ∗ 46
River ∗ 49
Testament ∗ 51
The Lovers of Rome ∗ 53
Rebirth ∗ 56

FROM *Blind Rain* (2008)

Wake ∗ 59
Rehearsals for the New Order ∗ 61
Flag ∗ 62

Nerval's Lute * 64
Blue Instrument * 65
Exile's Song * 69
The Return * 70
Will * 76

FROM *Peal* (2009)

Górecki * 79
The Invention of Song * 81
Body and Soul * 82
Ringtone * 84
A Diet of Angels * 85
Elegy * 87
Homage to the Ear * 89

FROM *The Visible* (2012)

Memoirs of the Five Senses * 93
Empire of Light * 95
Blaze * 96
My Mother's Closet * 98
People * 99
Privacy * 102
Play * 103
Milk * 105

FROM *Choir of the Wells: A Tetralogy* (2013)

Ink * 111
The Invisible Hand * 113
Benthos * 116
Pill * 118
My Death Space Dot Com * 120
Robitussin * 121
Homage to Sebastian Stenzel * 124
The Blindness of Needles * 126
The Unfinished Slave * 127

Elegy for the Spanish Republic ⁕ 128
Limestone ⁕ 130
Audubon ⁕ 131
The Lost Year ⁕ 134
Homage to Phosphorus ⁕ 135
Luminescence of the Oceans ⁕ 137

FROM *For the Lost Cathedral* (2015)

The Gate ⁕ 141
Advent ⁕ 142
Sleeper ⁕ 144
Lebensraum ⁕ 146
Cross of Nails ⁕ 147
Threnody ⁕ 149
Idolatry ⁕ 150
Harvest ⁕ 153
Tallow ⁕ 154
For the Lost Cathedral ⁕ 156

FROM *The Other Sky* (2015)

The Delta ⁕ 169
Flowerbed ⁕ 171
Runoff ⁕ 173
The City ⁕ 175
Victor ⁕ 178
Thomas ⁕ 180
Sea of Trees ⁕ 183

New Poems

The Invention of the Radio Telescope ⁕ 187
Keats ⁕ 188
The Interiors ⁕ 194
Blackout Starlight ⁕ 195
Bone ⁕ 202
New Moon ⁕ 209

The Sculpture Garden
    1. Eve (Auguste Rodin) ⋆ 211
    2. Hammering Man (Jonathan Borofsky) ⋆ 213
    3. Quantum Cloud (Antony Gormley) ⋆ 215
    4. Bronze Crowd (Magdalena Abakanowicz) ⋆ 217
    5. Night (Aristide Maillol) ⋆ 219
Furrow ⋆ 221

FROM *Radiography*
(1997)

Native Tongue

To glimpse it lounging in the red clay,
blind as a worm and skinless, shot through
with bluish veins and a craze of fibers,
any wonder we tend to conceal it.
To feel the full length of it, the appalling

ligament braided in our throat and bound there,
so tempting just to bury it in words,
and why not. The way it beats itself
senseless, flitting about like a bird
in a closet, what life is that. And whose.

Still you must confess: it's less disquieting
than going tongueless. And life enough
to rise up in spite of us, peering
over the rims of teeth, anxious to please.
God knows what possesses it to try,

as if it could tunnel back to some world
it lost, some day when it was little but
hunger and nonsense and the body tangled
in its root felt less intimate or strange.
Given time it became the odd sister

of our two hands, a kind of bridge between
the body and the air that walks it.
And we swore—it was all we could do—nothing
would tear this wick from the lamp of the skull,
this rude animal from a swarm of angels.

Homage to Szymon Laks

The flint, the shoe, the sip of water,
the hard currency of last effects,
the necessity, the razor, the broken cigarette,
the object itself unadorned and mute,
the wick, the lens, and him—what was he

in light of these things, a stick man
in zebra clothes and butcher hat, his life
boiled down to a stone at the bottom.
He too found it oddly barbaric:
the little flame of joy in his violin.

Still he kept it going, for want of other flames.
He was nothing indispensable,
as things are, though blessed, fit
to swell a mood or party, to animate a march.
Work, said the music, will make you free.

And how could he blame them, the ones
who cursed him, there, the Kapellmeister
of Auschwitz, him and the whole makeshift
of bad instruments and uncertain hands:
the rosin, the spit valve, the splintered reed.

No telling when the next shower of blows
would fall or why, if there were reasons
to drive them or if they fell merely
for the pleasure: art for art's sake.
Birds weaved over the crematorium.

From a distance they were a flock of needles
closing a rip in the sky's cloth.
And always the unearthly legacy below:
the lamp, the chimney, the illumined tattoo;
the pillow stuffed with human hair.

Each day without warning another soloist
lost, tearing out a hole in sound.
And he rushed like water to fill it.
That, after all, is what the living do.
Mornings when the sky was cloudless and bitter

he wanted to believe the music would save him,
and it did, though not without a measure
of luck and guilt and the fear that sent
some men to the wires, demoralized by hope.
Or so he said. The shame of living

is never to outlive it. There were days
in winter it took everything he had
to move his stiffened hands, to curl inward
over his violin, shivering, his white breath
rustling on his fingers like a flag.

Divorce

It seemed so unlikely, how the wind shattered
into little sticks and pieces, the green
lengths of limbs coming off at the shoulder,
and rooftops sizzling under sparks of rain.

Then the power as it died in our freezers
wet with meat; and the startling of clocks,
how they opened the black dials of their eyes,
listening: somewhere a tiny motor clicked

on in the family pet, quiet as glass
the way it trembled, and what we breathed
darted back into our bodies and gasped.
It made us feel so meager, so small-boned

and curious; even as the weather raised
our cube of rooms to its ear and rattled,
we never woke completely, but always.
And though the storm dragged over us, the world

grew strangely intimate, as if the more
it pried open with its hands, the farther
we would go and deeper, to feel it tear
our lives apart, skin from sleep, light from thunder.

North: 1991

In the euphoria that followed
the American air strike
when the New York Exchange soared

over the smoldering cities
and hovered there, a frail spire
aimed at heaven, I was driving

North, like so many who work
in town and live in the canyon.
It was the one road along the icy river

through the narrow tunnel
of my light, the radio cupping
a last match of news in its palm:

I live so close to nowhere.
I've driven this route ten winters,
and never was it so difficult

under the tallest trees,
ice-shagged, splintered,
holding up all of January

as if to give it back.
The highest branches rose
like the antlers of a startled elk.

There was no other way
but up, past the bent girders
over Cold Creek, through the small

fires of snow, layer after layer.
Winter's vault closed without a click.
Higher still where the road turned

into dirt and stone, tapering,
I got out to open the driveway gate
and felt my body grow tight

against the cold. There would be chores,
kindling to gather, a day's weather
in the satellite dish.

But for the time I stopped everything
to stand in the distance
of myself, turning white,

and could hear the thin ecstasy
of saws, the rise and fall,
a crackling in the hard wood.

The Possible

Once they were all we knew in the world,
the shapes of prayers and questions rising.
In radiant cribs, they curved up at the ends
of our voices. There was much to believe.
By a potted palm in the broken sun,

we felt them on our tongues like milk.
They slipped out of the names we gave them.
Once they rose in the wells of our bodies,
sprouted as hairs where the soil was darkest.
It was all we could do to keep them down.

Nights they backed away into the future
gazing at the body of the past, spread
themselves like a bride before a mirror.
We stood up too charmed to sleep and listened.
They made light of threats, promises.

When we cut them in two, each half shuddered
in a fierce dream, they gave praise to no end.
How we wanted it to go on that way,
the evenings we stripped like oranges,
the soft, declarative fist of the heart.

But already we owed our lives to days
that refuse to straighten but come back
drifting in their arc, broken by horizons,
bearing down where we bend to drink, mourn,
brace ourselves for the world's return.

Confederate Dead

Small comfort, to have survived your name
and body, given over to the false tints
of painted slides, though, as we are often
led to believe, a dead man could do worse,

as in one of those accidents of charity
when the images were sold cheap, for the glass
at the heart of their tragic sentiment,
thousands of photographic slides raised
into the roofs of greenhouses. Go there.

See for yourself. Impossible as it is
to make out the red translucent cloth
and fire, the fog of sleeves, to trace
the man where he stood among so many

past misfortune he must have seemed
a phantom to himself. You never know.
You too might look up some day at the sheer
sky through the center of his body.

It takes a forgetful mind to enter the past
completely, the way we eventually do,
in our dotage perhaps or still later.
Or like the invisible man shell-
shocked from all feeling in his arm.

This too is how to survive your life,
to draw blanks over an effulgence
of scallions, blood tomatoes, the thick green air,
to be made singular in a true sense.

Or if not to survive it, to consume it
the way fire consumes itself, concealing.
Denial is like that, however ceremonious
or slight. The past eats and is eaten,

though it sometimes helps to think of this
as mercy. And it is. It takes years
of sun to bleach a phantom arm or flag, to turn
the way a widow turns her grief to her child.

No telling who she looks through now.
It's a comfort to think the dead there,
though they were always closest as a hunger,
a sinking into warm glass, unshattered, clear.

Pomegranate
for L.K.

You could be turning it in your fingers like a planet.
A knife would do, if you're good with knives,
bracing the armored fruit in your hand.
A knife and a narrow gaze to guide it.
You brush a fly from your lip, quiet your breath.

Then there's the sound a vow makes when it shatters,
and the shallow fissure splits and reddens.
And all for this. A stain running out of a maze,
its honeycomb filled with dead bees.
Your hunger is a straight line, pinned and singing.

It's only now you realize what you craved,
how shyly you ripened into a panic.
As for the shiny rivulets of juice
you close your eyes to drink, who's to say
it was their freshness that drew you. All those times

you slipped your tongue into the bright tomb
the way a moth enters a jar of lamplight.
You know the place, how its mouth meets yours.
And now wherever you leave, it's winter.
You go to the window and wait, stare, turn away,

and the long night trails you like a gown.
Even in March as you return to all
your namesake, what flowers you see are the tips
of buried fingers, each red flame bursting
through the earthly crust, calling you down.

Radiography

Nights like this my body would open
the iron door of a deeper rest.
Snow falls in a shower of pins.

It lights up out of nowhere
in the glowing radius of our house.
And all around me, the little clicks

of appliances and hot pipe,
this year's hatch of winter fleas,
the way our room contracts into

the cold hours, the way it swells.
My sleep has never been so sheer.
My husband slips into bed late

and mumbles, pulls the sheet to his lips
with a moan that is part comfort,
part complaint. I think of him

as two people longing to converge.
He cannot resolve the shapes
of questions, disagreements, whatever

leans into the half that listens.
Tempting, to take our wakefulness
with us, to lie face-down

in our wild hair, hands buried,
fingers curved like a watch-
maker god at a small creation.

Not that I am any less
the stranger to my husband's work,
his solitude, but I can't stop seeing

that room, those books, his photos
of the failing lamps in bodies.
There are days they could be anyone's:

this feathery shade of veins,
the pale oval lake of the bladder.
There in its glass, a glint of scars.

Last night by the subway window,
I watched my tired reflection
give way to the emergent light

of Oak Street Station and briefly revived.
As a native I tend to keep
my distance, but there on the live steps

I listened to the tenor player
bite into his reed and solo,
wincing over the high reaches and god

if I didn't envy the body
inside his body. He comes down
most days with an Orphean resolve,

his face afire in its skull-cap,
especially deep into the ends
of phrases. It's as though the harder

he locks into the bright apple
of his sound, the more his breath
leads him, even as he shapes it,

raising up what his hands remember,
his black case gleaming with quarters,
eyes closed. Perfect health, my husband

once said, is a picture of night,
clear and starless, without fate.
What then does a body tell

anyone of the life it leads
into pleasure? Only a nonsense
of aches and wishes, a falling off

into memory and other bodies,
a shade younger perhaps, more faint,
wrapped in the thin fabric

of our looking. I never told
my husband how it is sometimes,
how old encounters reemerge less

as a past than the unresolved
shapes of promise after promise.
I never told my husband all

the palmist said of what she saw there
and who, or what she thought I wanted
in her care to leave things open.

In her young hands, my heartline
lay under the stitch of tracks
tunneling into the white ore.

It's something I do for myself,
my husband being further from such things,
skeptical. I like to believe

we agree unscathed in our slight
withholdings, not to mention
the desires we keep from ourselves.

Though they rise beneath my knowing,
trailing in the intricate music,
the idea of them precedes me.

Say you wake up some night stunned
in refrigerator light,
staring into the vestibule,

and realize how little thought
it took to carry you there:
already you grow too large to return.

When the door closes, your shadow
becomes the room you're in.
You walk back to bed, a chill

of milk clinging to your lips.
In my best dream, I am no less
blind: I close my eyes to kiss,

listen, to go forward in my sleep.
Or like Beethoven in his death mask,
to sink into a deep sensation.

I've seen my husband like that:
contemplating a word he's lost,
still groggy under the booth

of rain our bay windows make.
There's scarcely a nerve below
he would not turn down like sheets.

In my favorite *Twilight Zone*,
what I love most is the moment
of discovery, when the boy who gets

his one wish for x-ray vision,
so thrilled to see his girlfriend
whole, burns a channel of sight

past the brief arrival of skin
to the weird labor of her
physical heart. He gazes clear

into its chambers, though only
for a moment there, and through,
where suddenly we find ourselves

at the morning end of a mere dream.
We're a kind of radium that way,
outwardly serene, the bits of us

sparking under our eyelids.
It's how I picture the inventors
of heaven, the way they bow their heads

in a heightening of senses.
They are leaning over something
glittering in the dark, some plate

of water with the sky in it.
Never so clear as in that silence
before a big meal in winter;

just inches from their grateful teeth,
the cooked meat perspiring.
Who can condemn them for the world

they've made, the beautiful machines
of cathedral organs, that wine-
red glass and wax smoke? It sweetens

their bread to think of it: the idea
of a buried, more brilliant life.
They take it on their tongues,

douse the little flames there,
and mumble sleeplessly. To take
and be taken. Not to reject

the world, but to finish it
in their minds, to give it an end
as if it too were a body,

beautiful once and driven,
to hold it the way one body
holds another, how we hold our own,

looking down in bathroom showers
at the slow fuse of being alive.
These nights I lie still as glass

and feel my very cells divide,
alert to sleep or a husband's touch.
Mostly I drift off just this side

of dawn. The snow, if it snows,
turns clear in the black dirt.
Each cold seed is opening.

FROM *The Throats of Narcissus*
(2001)

Cruor Dei

As if we arrived through the blind extremes
of sleep, we opened our mouths, eyes closed,
and the priest laid on our tongues his coins
of bread, what we learned never to cross
with our teeth, never to rush, for at the heart
of each was God's nerve, burning and alive.

Then we washed it down with wine and Latin—
cruor dei, God's blood, the stuff I figured
flowed in everyone's body—what did I know—
though here was the glad horror of appetite
taking it in, and memories of other gods,
how they in their stories were torn apart,

exploding into the ten thousand things,
into the still-conscious body of names
for things, with every word a hint of blood.
It's how I picture crowning into the world—
through red water over rims of bone
into a little chaos of lights and gasping.

I like to think the blade binds as it cuts,
mother from child, that each solitude
ripens into a name for the other.
And as the mother looks down, her voice
is a braid of scar tissue between them.
It draws the child further into debt

he never resolves, not wholly, but sees
in the unlikely bodies of passersby,
in the man, say, caught on film, who keeps
bending back the car door, pulling a stranger
from a seat on fire—a birth of sorts,
though none is entirely his to repay.

It's only the trace, at best, a kindness
remade the way gods remake themselves
in our image, half-naked, their hands nailed
to some bare wall in sweltering Texas.
Their feet are vines crossing in the brick shade.
They would turn us all into mothers, grieving.

And among our children: debt and hunger.
Sometimes you feel them thinking, confiding
in the barely audible speech of twins.
In bad times they almost sound like hope.
Which they are. So many cuts, so many streams
of erotic letters welling up in the rift:

a lover says goodbye in the hazard lights
of an idling taxi, a pulse in the eye
she will never quite remember or forget,
not completely, and to live just this side
of completion is to turn further inward
the way a key of light turns in a gaze.

So it is with my father in his illness,
railing at the bolted apartment door,
cursing his wife for locking up his wife.
Or swearing he is the doctor again
with patients enthralled in another room.
He is the complicated child, the latch

lifting on an intricate cage. He scissors us
into broken flocks of memory and wish
which are his own body tearing apart,
though it is tough to say he suffers
the knowledge, our sense of what he was
or will be. It could be kindness too:

the bony dice of days stumbling through him,
the bewildering children who hold out
their shadowy bruises, too young to know
which wounds are serious—they all seem so
early on—or which ones simply clear up
with time, going clean in their own blood.

1979

When the train arrives, as memory must arrive
in its own country, the beaten breath
of the engine collapses into Berlin station,
and a man surrenders to the current of travelers,
each rising trance on the mechanical stairs,
to the echoing concourse and iron arch,

the place where hours behind him now
open out across a moat of traffic—it's midday
after all—and the flamed edifice
of the chapel sits, its public steeple bombed-through
and left for good, shamed like a boy
strapped in a chair: the indelibility of guilt

and rancor, the charred lip of the gash.
Disrepair is its own monument.
And it gets more that way, more stubborn
and unlikely, as all around it street-life rises
in bus-fumes and the scent of meat,
trains smoldering to the ravenous mouth

that will not close. When the Reich fell
the city shattered into four cities,
then two, as if some warped mitosis were going
backward, yearning for history's last
absorption, one cell gazing at the other,
sequestered in its unforgiving wall.

Swallowed through the cathedral door,
a stranger to churches let alone to the fire
that brings them down, he hears the accents thickening,
the black forest of the foreign tongue,
the air breathing him. He walks a bit,
flips through a tourist pamphlet, retracing

the impenetrable facts: the gutted ribwork,
stone face, bombed chapel of the human mouth.
He enters their language as it enters him,
the way bar-smoke enters a child's parka,
and the more foreign it seems the closer
the wind that brought him here, however blind,

where the horrors of trains cool in their stalls.
Silence too has a destination
in search of the body it might step into,
the border guard waving it through,
like sky into the tattered roof,
the idea of liberty into a captive brain.

Just yesterday he took a sleeper,
waking only to show his passport,
to catch a glimpse of the boarded window
thorned in wire, falling back
into sleep; behind him now
the iron shadow of the free world.

The Sirens of Los Angeles

All summer as the blacktop softens drugged
in an ether of smog and visible heat,
you hear the car stereos beat the air,
the bass throb of vans blooming at stoplights,
a shushing window and its flash of song.

Light burns on a fender in a sluggish tide
of fenders, the whole flammable basin now
littered in the oily scraps of sparrows.
I love this city, however long I soak
in the shadows of my shirt, in the dark

plumes of riot and angry script, a wash
of syringes under the pier. It's the dark
a singer leans her mike to, saying *no*
to the world the way a child says *no*.
Palms beat their shredded wings in the sun.

They too are waiting for the earth to move.
No word for the phone-pole repairman lashed
to his mast, a song blasting in his headset,
drowning the street in solitary music.
An ambulance parts the waters of our traffic—

one life, one life, it says—and the cars
wash back to bury its path. When the sun sets,
it trails a florescence of theaters
and tail-lights, the fresh stupor of children
streaked in purple; there's an art to forgetting

that oceans know, swallowing the day's pill
of fire. The floodlit heads on billboards lay
their smiles over the heads before them,
wave on wave of blind eyes and giant teeth.
Everyday the world is growing younger.

We could drive to the darkened crest and look back,
the city cracked open like a radio.
In the distance a living wire of sound.
Copters prick the alleys with their spotlights.
We could work our lives with wax in our ears

and fool no one: even in our sleep we hear
the echoes blossom in the throats of dogs—
or is it our own sleeping throats we hear—
each heart a bottle of blood impatient
for land and feasting, longing to be poured.

Oval
after De Chirico

How faceless their pathos, the ovals
of these heads, huge, smooth, hermetic
as eggs, and solemn, especially the man's
angled heavily on its neck, shelled
in sleep: his bluish and drooping fingers,

the folded tide of sleeves, the whole
human collapse dreaming, pale as stone,
while above him the muse looks down,
his body half-man, half-a-makeshift
of wooden bricks, glue, plates of iron,

the failed glimmer and scrap of a life packed
into his chest. Half-monument, yes,
though corruptible, blooming with pity,
his great disproportionate hand resting
kindly on a chair. Imagine what it is

to open your body's language
like a vacant plaza—that missing arm,
was it hacked away or merely unconceived?—
a fountain drying in the salt-white air.
For every night in his thin coat of meat,

the machination of his gut, exposed,
he becomes more of the world than the dream
remembers, more fiercely lodged
in the stubborn wire and glass of things.
Which is not a place apart from solitude.

Far from it. And the man knows this
as the uterine child knows her way out
into a still more singular life, pressed
through the wound of another's body.
See the hole in the block of the muse's lung,

that empty gaze of public statues.
The look he gives rises like a scaffold
over the face of stones and cruel time—
a muse-in-progress—which is lucky,
that he would make an expectation of loss,

a chalk-white room of physical silence,
closed, save for the door cracked
shyly behind, a thin black seam leading
forward or back—difficult to say
or know what walls face-off around them,

if the world is a tireless regress of rooms,
no final exit, no curtain's hem limned
in daylight—only a maze of interiors,
each no more inward than the next. But then,
the very notion has grown unbearable

to the man, his skin filling with the ebb
of radio and distant cars, a woman's hand
putting a polish on the heart's shell,
flush, as shells are, with rumor,
magnificent and hopeless as the sea.

Thelonious Sphere Monk

Take any solo session from the Riverside
years, those long trapped breaths of dissonance
like smoke, a holding back of fulfillment
that becomes just that, our glad and broken
contract; and you hear the great sad boulders

of chords thump into place, foundation stones
for later work, entire soaring tenements
of work. Difficult at times, the way he kept
everyone waiting, those hours he stumbled
through uncharted tunes, tape rolling, until

his stagger had a heart's precision to it,
a largesse of hands startled by choice.
Which is why, beyond the scarred edifice
of tone-clusters and uneven strides, each room's
waste of cups and ashes, beyond the nights

his strings soured in a New York basement,
there's a lightness here, a compulsion
to surprise. Less an end to silence
than a yielding to its wants, to the bloom
of poverty and water inside it:

sound as the hard fruit of deprivation.
And though you see him stab at the odd key,
his finger blunted like a cigarette,
it's not rage at a world slow to forgive
or understand, not merely; not the chronic

deafness of taxis and jail-clerks, the phony
drug charge that left him jobless; but more
a private joy working on its problem.
To raze and resurrect, to resurrect by razing.
There are moments he seems so thickly bound

in the black suns of his eyes, his face
bearded as a buffalo, mumbling in the shade
of a dark-felt hat. How better to inhabit
the pride of disappointment, to spark
against the corners, making a language

out of a failure to speak—though in time
failure became just that, a handful of days
he refused it all: the phone calls, his wife,
his health, his music. They block-and-tackled
his spinet through the high window of a cramped

apartment. Who was he to suffer fools,
let alone his own hands; and it came on
so swiftly: the thinning of his face
in the stream of silence. Soon his piano
too was a black chest of wire and dust.

And memory was small comfort. All his life
the giant spools of pleasure and tape flowed
in one direction: how he lived, he died,
the high gothic cathedral of his style
eroding, its stones condemned, windows boarded.

The Flies

In your little globes of shattered facets,
hands always miss. What's a hand
but a clumsy twenty-fingered thing,

a curse to ignite your hysterical fuse,
wings sparking, spitting light, zagging
from screen to screen, synaptic? Think

of the greedy pincers your world spins
into: terror's puny virtuoso, particle
and wave, fallout of the planet's

perpetual fission, perpetual surprise.
All our lives we watch you scribble
your mad epistles, punctuate our lampshades,

ripple our skins. Will we ever stop
slapping ourselves this way?
In siren-swoons of descending pitch,

you lower your minuscule chainsaws
through our trances. Cruel children,
I hear you in the lulls of abandoned meals.

Your eggs are the bird's caviar,
the ravenous ellipsis, clandestine periods
breeding periods. You are the pupil

flown free of its iris, the aqueous sparkle
of your thorax fierce with thirst.
Obsidian chip of the mind's arrow

sharpening down to no mind: you rub
your hands in silence, polish your eyes.
Then the sudden zipper in the air.

Dismantle your armor and what remains
but armor, platelets licked in black glue.
Together you are sputtering kernels

of petrified ash, thick pepper beneath
the sky's great hunger, impacted droppings
of angels, microsurgeons of the dead,

dizzy spell of the open wound. No sleep
for the tiny proboscis needling the sheen,
the blood that lights your hemispheric eyes.

The Throats of Narcissus

> The ego, captivated with its own making, its own history... lures consciousness, moment by moment, into a space that has no frame, no limit, and therefore no body.... it becomes bloated on an aesthetic that camouflages seams.
> —MARK F. KURAS

I

Call it a hole in silence: the bird
in this yard with the trill of a distant phone.
A tongue's needle shuttles in its throat.
Word without end, amen.

Then the sound of kids in a yard next door,
the boy's voice singing *charge.*
And they run up against each other's death,
every one of them swooning on the lawn.

Forever late—the dead—bound up
in a traffic of flies, black sparks
of the brain's fire. Overhead, a buzzing
of wires. Someone answer the phone,

they say. *Look world, I'm swooning.*

II

Picture Medusa, her head full of worms,
as if death were an excess
of life, a breathless canyon panorama.
Soon the air below turns to stone

you carve a face in. Your iris,
a mirror, lifts the mirror
from its rock, so now your every prospect
drags a lengthening path

like a father at his family tree.
The roots you draw are hands
reaching for the earth's core,
for its tiny period, *Eureka*, its atom,

and the blown sky that's buried there.

III

Not that blood alone made him restless,
but how it pulsed on the ocean
of his pillow like a stranded flashlight.
The heart a throb of option;

waves the world turning its insides out,
lathering a white nothing at the core: *if
you want to reach me you have to go through
the hungry mouths of door after door, to meet

your evening in its drunken robes and hair
like fire, its whorish sympathies dripping
in shipwreck and pills.* And so he turned away,
though no less into shipwreck, and pill,

to swell the heavy boredom of the sea.

IV

Then the blood woke in him as a pool
of water he just stepped out of,
and he held the pool in one hand
like a magnifying glass, when no sooner

it darkened to a wound, the dead eye
in an empty camera. And then it was

the place he baptised his children,
and they drank it up like little sponges—

such tender criminals. No matter how hard
he squeezed there was always more,
the flesh soaked in it, and so in fear
he left his body—they all did—

as if it were the whole story . . .

V

. . . as if light shone through the tiny rips
in the world's cloth. You see in a newspaper
the girl's face that disappeared
from the sheriff's parking lot last noon,

then the long straight line
of no news, that arrowing horizon
they laid her body in. The poison darts
of flowers have put the earth to sleep.

In Auschwitz once a group of prisoners
put God on trial and found him
guilty—it took what candles
they had—as if gods and men went

to their deaths together. Like lovers.

VI

The sins of cigarettes are hubris—
Vantage, Merit, True—as if their names were
the breath words ride before they ride.
In a film a man pulls a string

of diamonds out with his teeth, right out
of her body a trickle of stones.
Smoke goes through their pockets like money.
Then he is the bell-rope rising

in her tower, her voice the weight
that grips and pulls him. In each a nameless
calling: *come see the peep-hole*
in its dark confessional, be the ice

weeping in its mouth, absolved.

VII

And when he saw the river in his eye
and fell in as if he were everything
the river lost, a sky-thing with a god-
like absence, he could not know the body

he fell into was the one he left . . .
until it came: the tremor of plates
in their cabinets, God's tanks
as they broke through the city's heart

and deeper, rolled in the eyes
of televisions into the curfewed streets.
Like children, graves dropped open their mouths,
whole choirs of them. And the bold

white shirt fluttered on his back.

FROM *Cinder*
(2003)

The Fall

I

We have come this way before,
my father's body laid out like one horizon
we cannot cross, gone soft with all
the suns it swallowed.

I am stepping into a paper boat.

What is it that leaves in pieces. Cleansed.

We wake, my father and I,
in the middle of my sleep.
Where there is no sleep, there is nothing but.

This ground, this cloud, calling.

II

Day eight and he surfaces faintly,
his eye opening now and then
with its portal to the mind's dark,
the enormous wilderness, listening,
sending out an invisible tremor.

It thrills us like the sighting
of a whale breaking daylight.
Never have I felt so close to the shine,
so drawn to the living circle,
laid bare to the quiet claim it makes.

I'm at a loss now what to tell him,
my words repeating as if they dissolved
at once, each sound set down
in the water of his silence.
I hear the talk of other rooms.

In time we are indistinguishable
from what we cannot say.
It binds one life to the next,
this patch of white falling into white.
The respirator crests and surges.

We hold that sensation just long enough
for his eye to glaze,
the mighty fish in him drawing air
and diving, bearing light
to the starless reaches below.

III

In my closet waits a black coat
dark as a path under ocean air
through the middle of the night.

Sky salts the body where it wanders.

IV

There is a day beside a river
in Idlewild, California
where my father laid a hand
over a bump I got, a head welt
he christened *little goose egg,*
and I ached a while, stunned,
though not without a shadow of pride.

After all I was with child now,
the compress of his palm turning
then to the trace of a palm,
a phantom crown from the man
who seemed to me a founding
father of the world,
a child's world, granted,

though even now as he falters
on the brink of something vaster,
I see the day simmer
like pavement doused in gasoline.
It dazes me still, this shine
of blood inside me, as if to bruise
myself were to polish something

older than the names we carry.
If only I could lay my palm
over the eye of his wound
as if to blind it, to take its power away.
Anything to answer this
constant swelling, to leave there
a phantom hand, still as ice.

V

Tear down the curtains
and the fever of day upon them.
Tear down the scrim of sky
with its ragged hole of sunlight.
Tear down the sun, a shock
of stars scattering in its wake.
Tear down the night's fabric,
the cruelty of loss and behind it
the terrible charity of greater loss.

Tear down the pole star
and let the others come undone
sparkling like bees.
Tear open a place for the moon
to rise, for the fist,
the skull, the flower of it.
Tear out the image of the moon
in our eyes and give it back.

Give it all back, the field
of broken teeth, the bees,
the hungry patterns they make.
Make an offering of molecules,
of the pinched stars
that are our bodies.
Make a beacon of this heap
of scraps and fire.
Let us beat the black door of the sky
and deliver what we've made,
what we've torn, this minor mountain
of horror and seed, this compost
of worlds, this father,
this welter, this sting, this son.

VI

When I sleep I wear my father's face,
his blind amazement, the zero
of his open mouth. I am calling out
after him, the way one calls
to a taxi deafened by rain.

The weary, the damned, the smitten,
the deceived, the prayer unanswered,
the long lines of their descent,
in each a little earth, returning.
The pulse, the pride, the mercury, the snow.

In my chest I carry him fallen there.
To breathe hard is to hear
the shush and tumble—I do—
the sound of air erasing itself,
a car radio entering a tunnel.

Rope

Who was it who first believed
each strand of our experience
is coiled into the long ropes
of the brain, that no matter
how many dawns break their waves
of light over the eye, we manage
to hoard it, all of it, and if
only we could wire some charge
into the right place, we are there,
born across the frightened
sheets of a mother's blood,
entire, having broken the water
of our denial, without the current
sweetness of memory and loss;
and to test our faith, we will live
our whole lives over, and burn
both ends of this fuse to the center,
remembering and not remembering,
and bearing in mind the difference,
and not bearing, until we come
to the moment the wire dreams
its own descent, that little
charge of pure illusion,
and its laying down of ropes—
who can blame us after all—
in the phantom ropes we are, we are.

The Island City of Dmitri Shostakovich

> If my hands were cut off, I would continue
> to write music with the pen between my teeth.
> —DMITRI SHOSTAKOVICH

For months now I have crawled inside these preludes
and fugues, the color of night's icy structures
turning to water, polishing the silence.
There's a light sleeper just beneath the surface,
the sound in his head a threnody sweetening.
The very scent would melt a tyrant in his tomb.

Once Dmitri's desk drawer savored its privacies:
toy parodic marches full of spit and wobble,
a child's elegy, a Hebrew prayer. Stave after stave
tiny thorns and blossoms clustered on their stems.
It became his vital crime, this life, the drawer
drawn open like the jaw of a dreaming boy.

However stiff the vodka in his cup,
he felt the occasional season of tremors
tugging at his cheek, tightening the mask.
Those years you took a man to the toilet
to crack a joke, he said; you flushed the water to whisper
the gag, then laughed softly into your fist.

It's as if his body had a stranger in it,
an inmate huddled at the oven of his heart.
Come winter each boot print to his door
was a large ear filling up with snow.
Darkness too was white this time of year.
Dmitri slept with his bags packed beside him,

scared of the secret knock of police,
not that he would escape, only that he might
slip away in silence, the way sleet slips

into the Neva at night, without stirring
the uneasy peace of his wife, his children,
their sheets a quiet ruffle of wings.

City of islands, river fractured, charmed,
the brachia of its palace gates so shocked
with gleam they seemed suspended in the air.
Even St. Isaac's gilded cupola, emboldened
with the weight of its treasure, was one
cold burgeoning sun arrested in its flight.

And there, beside a northern bridge, the four horses
reared and grappling the sky before them
as if they would leap right out of their bronze—
the whole of it built on a swamp of human bones,
skeletons swept from the founding scaffolding
to light the crystal ceilings of the place.

However thick the cinder-block tenements,
factory smoke, curbsides heaped with soured snow,
however heavy the new Russia resting on its stilts,
a fabled frailty survived, each spired confection
plagued with cracks, weather burnished, flood prone,
the skies a frosty compress over a fevered gold.

You can hear them in the brooding momentum
of his bass, the patient rage and impacted stairwells,
a basement maze thrown open to the notes
that sketched his name: D-S-C-H: the brassy stretch
of a figure so long repressed it hungered
for refrain: D-S-C-H. That too had fever in it.

Such heat for a shivering sparrow of a man
skittish with fire and outstretched hands.
Such an enormous weight released he would have the dead

quaking in their sleep, rising to the final movement
as if it were their names buried in his.
Go there. Check the numbers on the headstones,

the bodiless effigies of friends gazing back.
There's a strength in the strings' lower reaches
that wears at this bitterness, a resolve
in the rock with the lily on its chest,
the sex of lime trees powdering the gravel,
their wind-bent spines bursting into song.

River

While we never step in the same stream twice,
    the same story as we know it,
        the same dark room we wake and rise to,

so too there's a river we never leave,
    which is why, as I checked my watch that morning
        before we drove to put our cat to sleep,

I felt a heavy current at the backs
    of my knees, an invisible water
        on my arms, my chest, over my head,

and at the bottom of it all our cat,
    oblivious, walking a crooked line,
        attending to her ritual of meat and pills.

How deceitful we felt as we carried her
    trusting body newly groomed, laid it out
        on the steel table, committing ourselves

to the final motions: the humming shaver
    over her leg, the needle's slow insertion,
        a bead of blood in the gradual syringe,

and her eyes, now milky with age,
    sealing up as her neck wilted, death's
        white blossom in my unfamiliar hand.

It's as if some shine lay buried
    in the details, in the cold tray
        of sterile silver, the bright cloth

and gloved assurance so vivid inside
    the shy confusion of our mercy.
        Such power in a final day it seems

an overdose of life, a flooding
    of the open eye. No wisdom
        could prepare us for the prick and wonder,

how her gaze would narrow as if in pleasure,
    the way I half-expected to feel her ghost
        flitting through me, though I never did,

the body released, we say, though oddly weighted,
    like a mirror the night had fallen
        into, cleared of its last ripple of breath.

Testament

Almost winter and the groundskeepers are firing
    blanks into the trees,
scattering a nuisance of grackles from the branches—
    enough, say the guns,
of excrement and birdsong, and the sudden sight

is futility: great fistfuls
    of black confetti, the way they soar out shrill
with panic and return
    as if history would take them back, blowing
its leaves onto the trees again.

And with each return a storm of words falls
    into the limbs' antennae.
They are drawn into a woman's story,
    a woman's voice,
in her throat a nervous gathering of wings.

She was a nun, flightless in her robe and habit,
    pale under the scorch
and stare of a foreign sun, of a day men bound
    her eyes in burlap,
led her through a hole in the quiet planet.

For every profanity they put
    her through—these men who keep revisiting
her sleep—she feels profane
    to speak it, to go down that trail of burns
to the core of the disaster.

Which is more than any act at the center,
    the torturous
logic of pliers and knives, more than the open
    mouths of wounds
welling up with unspeakable life.

Beneath the scavenging aftermath of birds
    feasting,
she knows a silence that is a parody of mercy.
    It bears a head
without a face, an inability to forgive.

She opens her mouth and birds fly out.
    They are a flock of hooks
in the sky's fabric. To remember is to be wholly herself.
    Almost dark. She opens her mouth
and the trees inhale.

The Lovers of Rome

Say it is true, what the clouds imagine,
His apparition boiling from a cluster
of angels wingless in their troubled flight,

writhing to keep His holy weight afloat.
As Adam relaxes, God pins His eye
on the gift of living just beyond His grasp.

We can never know the long nights that stained
the painter's brush, if he dreamt of boys
dipped in amber, a palette of the boldest

minerals and berries, and yes, time.
Always more time on his back, more lamplight
hung in the scaffolding that held him.

What he conjured in his solitude—
the cadavers he opened like little mansions,
the figures he revived, those lovers of Rome

lifted high into the drying plaster—
they would stun the current of eyes below.
Such is the audacity of the place,

to perfect a vital stillness, the flames
of rock along the fluted colonnade,
flagstones strong as the floors of rivers.

Even the numinous scraps of fabric
blushing over the body's shame hover
with animal astonishment and stress.

There's something here on the cusp of waking,
some eye poised to open underneath us.
People walk softly and cough, leave their change.

They cannot exhaust the flesh they see.
Freakish, how art eats up the empty spaces,
these walls like skin so thoroughly tattooed,

needled by a hand at every anchor.
You would swear the room had swallowed the man
who in turn grew larger than the room.

So it is with any lover's image
watering the seams of the body it is in.
God's mirror shines in the fountain of His garden.

Say there is no other earth than this,
the ravenous dream of the dream-deprived.
Say that we too look up, year after year,

that we wake odd hours on a chapel bench,
parched, sore and chosen, breathing dust. Soon
the ripe fruit comes falling through its shadow.

Blades of birdsong are whittling away the trees.
There is a comfort even in the voice
of temptation, singling us out, calling our name.

And what is more tempting than a painter's
reply, to gather what he knows of gardens
and the severed corpse, of arcane fibers

gripping the bone, to bind them into lives.
Yours. Among the weightless and bemused.
If there is a self-portrait here, a secret

point of view, let it be the stray guardian
turning away, his face to the ceiling,
his fingers smeared in the cobalt of heaven.

He keeps plunging his hands back in
like birds at the busy ends of his arms.
How he longs to walk right through the plaster.

He keeps scouring his palms, or trying,
each over each like pieces of silver.
If only sky could rinse the sky away.

If one man could bear such theater
above him, beaming down, such black bile
and broken sleep, if he suffered as much

under waves of fever, with the lust
that turns like a giant wheel of rain,
what you see is the best of him pushing back.

To perceive it takes a certain distance,
the way the figure in a mirror seems
more wholly conceived, more self-possessed

than the one we inhabit. Or stranger still,
how we slip skin to skin in the puzzle
of another's arms, taking shape there,

however shyly, as they too take shape.
Who would not want to conceive a body,
not simply the bloodless shepherd of clouds

but something flush, polished, watched and cared for,
no less of the planet than marble or chalk.
Who would settle for mere flashes of hands

and legs, winged in shadows, our true faces
blind to themselves, our true backs trailing
a mystery behind us. Waiting to be touched.

Rebirth

What is it in the dawn of rain
that coaxes sleep from its cranial cove.

You ask the way the rain asks,
grappling at windows, veining the dark.

What is it in the softening panels
of your roof, in the widow veil of starlight

under no star, the burrowing body
in its bed sheets, the burrowing heart in its chest.

Could it be a steadiness comes over us
in the midst of all that coming apart,

the sound of prayer beads worried from their circle.
Never have you felt so cradled

in the luster of your mooring,
so narrow in the slip that rocks you blind.

Could it be the tiny stemware
of a million nameless christenings.

Your house leans its prow behind you—
you who give in to your appetite, who hear

in the rain the leafy-crackle of a long
awaited approach—the Lord giveth,

the Lord stealeth away—so long you wait
you take it for departure.

FROM *Blind Rain*
(2008)

Wake

One day now since my father last tried to speak,
since the outer provinces of his body shut
down like small cities when the power goes,
just the enormity of starlight to guide them
on their cold journey into dawn. I am writing
at the edge of the other half of life, the part
without my father in it; I feel the strange

sure pull of the earth I walk here,
the polish of the grass, the distance between me
and my students who look up and wait
for my first questions, knowing so little
of my life, just as I know so little of theirs,
only a poem at a time to hold us together
like children before a fire in the woods.

These months I have heard him steadily
fading in my telephone, his breath gone
short, just the occasional brush of wind
and language, here and there an angry stutter
and release, the little sighs that resign themselves
to his own deep and smoldering basin,
his own coastal reaches tossing in their tides.

The living too leave their ghosts behind.
And his, clearly, always the first to rise.
Somewhere a fork beats a metal bowl;
a strip of bacon crackles like paper at Christmas.
These days moving from room to room
I feel the shadow of this house begin
to lengthen, to feed the other pools of dark.

It's a mystery still, how vast the valley
inside a body. Blood. It's what you hear
when you cover your ears, that far surf
where life first sprouted its legs and crawled

ashore to dry its tail in the morning sun.
It's what sparks beneath a small syringe,
a red gem brightening in a sting of air.

It's what calls you to a father's ragged breathing.
Somewhere a lung fills with water.
Somewhere a great and weary muscle
beats the tender drum of the sky.
It's the father who knocks on the door
at daybreak, the knock that says, it's time
son, rise and shine, it's time to go, it's time.

Rehearsals for the New Order

The courthouse is empty now, ablaze
with holly, wreathed and ribboned for the season,
standing firm against a thrill of breezes,
the grinding arcs of stars, grackles crazed
and dizzying the turret, the drunken hair
of winter gardens at its feet, while inside
great mahogany walls, no judge presides,
no footstep polishes the marble stair,
no clerk turns to the window, rubs his eyes
and turns again: time to free the animals
into the evening air, to let them howl
from yard to yard; somewhere a solitary
stem of smoke blossoms from a chimney;
an old man watches his money wither
and rise, then fall again, over and over
without peace; somewhere a nation moves;
the blades of ships are opening the water;
somewhere a small tree brittles in its silver
and glass; all night we feel the sky there
listening, the tap that drips like tiny hooves.

Flag

These nights in all their smoke
and armor, the great concussions
of bad faith thumping the horizon,
the epileptic flash inside the cloud
giving it depth, reach, weight to pull
as we move about our drowsy city,
I keep seeing my mother's room
at dusk, small, fading, lit by the ice
of television glass; how brief a life,
how long the hours, how fretful
the mother who picks the spice
grain by grain from a plate of meat,
who presses her palms against her eyes
as if to bury the world in the world.
Any wonder I too turn the pages
of my linens, bathed in ink,
that I sink my face in my pillow
and read. And whose world is it
that leans so close to blow out
the stray candles of my words,
to pare the evening horror down
to human size, to the crumpling
sound of spring rain; whose hand is this
that cracks the window of a book,
its Buddha hemmed in flags of fire,
a hub in the mind's wide *wheel* of fire.
Be in the world but not of it,
says the book—or is it the other way—
be lodged in the ring of flames
so deep there's no retreating.
I could be somewhere between this
wakefulness and another country,
in the no fly zone of near-sleep
where ceilings buckle, sigh, click
into place, where the clock bleeds

a little nightlight, humming,
over and over the wind gives
its briefing to the alders,
and who am I to talk, I say,
as if God burned the letters that we sent.
My flag is not my flag
draped on the face of a tyrant statue.
Its colors are no brighter
than a song I sang badly as a boy.
No song, says the world, *not now.*
No mooning over a troubled covenant.
No song for the beast of the literal
heart thrashing in its irons.
And then it comes to me:
my father's weariness at the end
of day, eyes glazed, his body
bearing what I could not fathom.
It is 1954; somewhere still
ash settles on a village in Korea.
Bombs shake the Nevada sand.
Birds drop out of the sky in cinders.
Be in the world but not of it,
says the body, the eye, the ring of flames.
My father blankets the grass,
tunes the somber radio and falls
asleep, drowned in violins—
hello in there, we whisper—
that gentle snore like a cleft chain
dragging across the ocean floor.

Nerval's Lute

> My sole star is dead,—and my constellated lute
> Bears the black sun of Melancholia.
> —GÉRARD DE NERVAL

Walk into the black of Nerval's lute,
into the body of the instrument,
its choir of shivers, the gut of it lit
with language not quite spoken here, not yet,

with the loss of something so immediate
the memory eluded him: the mother,
the river, the woman who spurned him, not
them alone, but how they all would figure

into letters that he wrote the world.
And the world spoke in turn, though drenched
in music, in mercies of decaying pitch,
a foreign tongue which seemed the very will

embodied, the dream exhumed: everywhere
the votive candles of the lilies, the hills
of burning brass, the sky's acetylene stare
returning his those final days, his mind

in such a crushing fever the dead looked on
in pity, reached out even, so in the end
however disinherited the wound
of the open throat, however long

its stretch into the burial of suns,
it was a darkened happiness that dawned
that morning, that took him in its hands,
its human hands, and cut the body down.

Blue Instrument

It's come, the trembling time,
that tireless white noise moving
through her body, my mother's hands
so fitful in their quiet room, no music,

no books, no natural light, nothing
to graze her nerves with its cautious beauty,
save her ancient chest of drawers
watching over like a father. A curse,

she says, how they cannot understand.
In her mind a boat with no one in it
cast out over the night's lake, cloaked in fog.
Her face a lamp buried in the haze.

To speak of faith is to fail her, and yes,
I say, now is when you need it most.
The words go somewhere, I know; I see them
sink through the still waters of her eyes.

All I can do to take her hand in the strangeness
of my own, to be the fog around her,
the godless place inside the word *God*,
the wind of an arm, coming on, letting go.

Somewhere my mother stopped playing
the piano and began to play the radio.
Even as her fingers knotted up with age
she felt the radio waves inside them.

Her whole body was one big radio,
first with the clarity of one song,
then two, then a blizzard of the many
ivories and voices, the all too sweet

and adolescent growl, the news flash
patter from the burning cities,
the chant of the blood beneath it all
thumping the floor like an angry neighbor,

the song of the worried keys, the rifled wallet,
the fool's joy in rainy weather, the hymn
of praise she buried in a book, here, now,
the one she clings to and will not open.

Once I took my trouble to the river,
thinking how my mother's world
had contracted around her, its lord,
as surely as her body clung to the staff

that was her suffering. I took my image
of her on the throne of her bed
saying, don't go, don't chicken out now,
which is what I inevitably did,

or what I suspected of myself,
for I was part of that conspiracy
that could never be there, not fully.
Don't go, don't go, the echo marked time

as I went, thinking the river might calm
the mind with its constant leaving,
the cold amnesia of its shine, a flock
of clouds grazing upstream as I gazed

lost between a sense of solitude
and the weariness of traveling, always
with that one far voice, that one room
she could not leave for fear of being alone.

No, she says, to the pill, the spoon,
the prayer, the fever, no to the sun
that hems a nervous curtain,
no to the cries of boys in a distant yard,

to the son's cruel talk of hope
and weather, no to the voice
that is not there, to the thousand ears
of leaves around her, no to the trip, the fly,

to the hired help arriving, sleepless,
worn by the call of a small gold bell,
no, she says with her head like the blind
musician sinking into a soft chord,

the kind of no that says, yes,
it's here, stronger than expected,
the bass of it opening up beneath you,
the hush that takes you with it as it fades.

I used to dream of a blue instrument,
a dry breeze strumming the harp of the ear.
My mother too was there, the one
I never had, the musical mother,

her ghost rising out of the actual throat.
To think she lay there all along
inside the grip of bones guarding
its vital rhythms, inside the flush

of embarrassment or panic.
The unlived life is a far cry

from anywhere, a city on its floating docks,
its ships like constellations

over the breathing waters—the kind of stars
I steer by, even now as I think of her,
as I eat, sleep, move about,
forever losing my place in the sky.

Exile's Song

A boy lays his hands on the backs
of his mother's as they float
over the keys, over the startled
water of a dead man's music,
its small waves and minor scale
exhaling the way the sea exhales
though not without a soft strength,
the kind that nightly eats the shore;
the shadows of the mother's fingers
darken slightly as they touch
the living hand, so stiff, she tells
herself, unsure above the shallow
current—it's all leaving her,
she thinks, the lather, the pulse, the art
of moving with it, but she plays
this once, this final time, if only
to encourage the boy—and who can
blame her—the islands of his flesh
over hers, until she becomes
that place, for the moment, that hand
between the dead and the living,
between sky and the other face
of sky, as if it were the music
of the warm surge, its widow's lace,
that brings a child into the world.

The Return
in memory of Giles Mitchell

As if the world we wake to,
glowing at the seams, were more
loyal than the one we leave,
more compelled, returning,
true, we say, as of a crime
or arrow, the path it takes,
the deadlier the truer,
the vision of a star pinned
and burning as the star goes out.

One more sleepless man at dawn
puts down his revolver,
closes it in his chest
of drawers. Its weight is that
of the moon sliding down,
an ache withdrawing
into the ephemera of days
to come. He chooses
with every breath and so lives

the burden, *free,* renewing
his allegiance step by step.
Who am I to presume the world
has a thing yet to tell him?
Still I want to say something,
as we all must, to recover
what it was that made life
the child he swore to spare, to care for,
to leave his minor fortune.

To recover, as in *the body
recovered, the gold bullet
of the sun, all good things received
and covered, shrouded in light.*

Long ago tomorrow was everything to me.
I loved it the way a small room
loves an only window,
the farthest reaches, the fever
of daylight as it rises and falls.

What is it to be so loosely in your skin,
so ill-defined who knows
what's there to give away?
Once, every wind blew its spiced and drunken rumors
through me. If I talked in my sleep,
it's just that I wasn't sure
if I was listening. Long ago
I loved the future the way a wick
loves the fire that eats it.

And so my first, my particular
flame, the girl whose bewildered
self emerged in the slow
shapes of deep water swells,
the kind that never break.
If not charity, then her distant
sister, that tentative step
and the sound it made, my ear
pressed to the rising sternum.

Not without our gaffes and stumbles,
those nights entangled
in the backs of cars,
the petty words that hung in the air
waiting for a mouth
to cover them up.
And all around us a wreath of crickets.
Going out, we called it,
the way a light goes out.

To throw a life into the life
you choose, into the one who chooses,
the mirrored mirror of the physical
eye, into the swift of not quite
knowing who, what, where
choice ends, the sea begins;
to make yourself a false promise
and watch the tidal rip of it
draw back into your aging eyes—

this too is one of those mornings,
how the surface of the screen
reappears at the movie's end,
though something more terrifying
is beginning and we know it,
something rising out of the body
looking down now on the plain
strangeness, the singularity,
of the body, our body, of anyone's body.

As children we could hardly look
to see our president wave, so slowly
pulled in his long convertible
splitting the cheer of a day in Texas.
Then that sound like a slapping
of books. The spits of flesh.
Over and over we watched it
as if the recurring footage might
reconcile a nation with its facts.

Anger, yes, and disbelief,
the blur of objects held too close,
but beyond that: it was the first
I saw my teacher as someone
more, history's orphan, closer
to a child, unsteady as she broke

the news, her voice so small,
so soft at times it seemed
she was speaking to herself.

Foolish as it sounds,
it was just then beginning to dawn,
not simply the flash of one broad day,
how it lowered a silence
the size of a cathedral,
but more: how the world that shook
my teacher and her brittle English
was, if not our world,
the frightened one we would inherit.

The first I heard of Vietnam
it was a television show my parents watched.
Me too as the time advanced,
as it fell in bolts of black cloth
over a family down the street.
Every morning the sun rose
on the jungle of who we thought we were,
what we lost, what we had become.
Even those who returned never returned.

What is more certain than the thing
of which we know so little?
Limousines drive the fresh dead
in caskets draped in fields of stars
so that the sky would drink up
the phantoms in their boxes,
calling them home, we say,
as if it were the living who live
as exiles in the new world.

Imagine the Tibetan children,
how the New China instructed them

to bring what each had killed
to school: it was their work:
one point for a fly, two a mouse,
three a bird, a cat, and so on,
anything to break the life cycle
of the heart, how they threw it
into each small suffering thing.

I don't pretend to know the luminous
emptiness of what they see,
to have what it takes to step lightly
through the labyrinth of bardos
and back. Still I admire anyone
who, as the story goes, chooses
to return to life, whose kind ghost
reawakens, an infant in the flesh
of day, flushed and crying.

And looking down on all sides, the joy
of arrival. So quiet, this joy,
so easy to dispel with the need for joy,
I am reluctant now to speak of it.
For those who wait, it seems to come
from a great distance, returning the way
a father does after years at sea,
his too large coat and the hat he holds
doused in the indigent rain.

True, we say, as of one returning
but also of the eros of return.
Why is it always one woman now
balancing the scales of my bed?
My north, my wife, my nocturnal iris,
each night a little smaller
in her skin, she whom the curtain

turns to in its blindness.
So quick to fall asleep.

A gift, how faithfully she takes
the dishevelment of days
inside, expecting just as surely
to return, as if she saw it: the future
had arrived without closing its eyes,
its distance, as if anything so
shy, so alive, could be
before her, still and breathing,
calling her name.

Will

To the locusts that blur the lyres of their shells,
I leave my blindness at the end of day.
To the distant whistle of the train at dusk,
I leave the smoke in a girl's hair.
To days I dipped my body in, I leave my only shadow.

To the gravel road where it crackles and spits,
to the fluster of the wheel, the brake,
the broken shoulder, its buckle and curve,
to the long labor of the open eye,
I leave one lush confession.

To the pincers of ants dismantling a bird,
I leave the bitter patch at the tip of my tongue.
To the porch light haloed in a scribble
of moths, I leave my boyish appetite.
To the hymn, the yawn, the three in the morning,

I leave the warmth of the engine
as it settles and purrs.
To the empty page beneath me where I lie,
I leave the weight of ink above.
To the hole that is my throat, I leave the flesh around it.

To the dream I can't remember,
I leave the one I won't. To my father's memory,
I leave the bread crumbs of my name.
To the body that follows a body to its grave,
I leave the seagull's laughter.

To the bride who says goodbye to the mirror,
I leave the cold face of the mirror.
To the one who reads, I leave the fire.
To the quiet brightening behind me as I go,
I leave the quiet to come.

FROM *Peal*
(2009)

Górecki

The slowly sweeping wheel of dust and iron
is not the upended carriage with no place
to go or call its home. Clearly we are somewhere
just to the south of something so embodied,
let us call it home. Let us call it a city
pocked with the aftermath of too many nights
to make a passage of, too many rattled
windows to settle in their grooves, however
washed in the sweets of lilacs and small street fires,
the occasional waft from the morning bakery.
It's here where the arc of the symphony
begins, out of the black bricks of Warsaw,
the gradual rise an enormous brood, the bass
viols, heavy, yes, though no less bowed,
glacial as a passage in a difficult book,
a book full of breath and the light it stretches
to extinction, a book you press to your chest
to feel the heat of your body slowly melt
the jacket and its pages, a book passing
into winds to lift you out of bed, to rake
the vagrant leaves across your roof. A winter
breezes through the large and hollow gate,
through the arc that is the shape a stone throws,
an all too sluggish siren bearing the heart
on its gurney, rising and falling, rising and falling.
A sun crowns the statuary horizon,
above the organ feet that walk up the dark
into the gabled room of belated song.
Always another ambulance to trail
the long and diminishing thread of hope
into ruin. And as we lie in bed,
we follow it, and what it follows. Even
the sigh of not knowing would have us
go on, the weary quietude that falls
to hypnotize the great symphonic wheel.
Even the part in the music where the flames

subside, the chapel in a spirit cloud
of smoke and rosin. Even the body's
diminuendo, the fading breath that waking
brings, the slowing pulse. First the bodies,
then the names: that's the way it is
with history. The sheer numbers darken
heaven's page. The red iron of a city's
carriage spins in the air. Part of the power
of what we hear is the sense we revisit
a place we never knew. Moved, we say.
In the way of blood, air, hand, stomach, eye.
As if even the respite of song is action,
its silence no less. Even the bend and reach
of architecture that rises out of the smolder
and back, even the legs of the arc that return
the way the sun returns to a black well,
its trespass quiet, slow, a ghost, a coin,
a wish gone deep as the day grows old.

The Invention of Song

Not the face, the human face,
floating in its crippled spoon;
not the needle where it drinks
night after night; neither the watch,
the blood, nor the gold in hock,
the world liquified to small bills
passed under the broker's jail;
no little crime of sweat that breaks
the child's lockbox of the body;
not the courage of the dour road
where it blisters into rough stone;
or the craze of the eye regarding
itself, the obsidian crystal;
not the mockery of the beast lung
bursting through its two blue doors;
or the shriek of birds glorified
with fear; not the pitch, the rock,
the ship of deaf sailors save one
lashed to his mast; not even the gash
of stars, the song, we are told,
too sweet to bear; but something
more, always more, the moon
in the wave, the animal, they say,
running in the Siren's veins,
the squall in the breach that calls
you out, mast or no mast, that grips
the buried shield of the sternum
as if it were the world's shield,
as if the heart dropped its massive
rope to hear, there, drowned in fog,
the sudden distance of its name.

Body and Soul

Where to find a cab in the morning dark,
where a quarter, a phone booth in the rain,
what to make of this night and the wreck
it lifts out of the harbor, out of the known

side of the mirror, to sink again each dawn.
To lift, the way the saxophonist lifts
the head of his exhausted tune, the lantern
in his bronze hands giving off what light

it can. He cannot count the times now
he played this ballad, this *Body and Soul,*
all the love-drunk versions he made new
and not new, the borrowed air that spilled

through nameless hands before him, that passed
out over smolders of laughter in a place
like this, over the clink of soiled glass
again and again. More than knowing this piece

by heart, this home key drifting up one step
to lead him burning to the bridge and back.
More than the weary man who will not sleep,
who cracks open his chest like a fake-book

to read the barest measures of the past.
There will always be a dim lounge, a corner
in this waste of dishes, where the soloist
seals his eyes, expanding. Always a minor

liberty startled by the sound it makes.
He breathes a bit, takes the lip of his horn
out of his mouth, to clear a quiet space
for the brush and cymbal, who yield in turn

a deeper quiet. And the upright goes down
softly now, though bold in what it asks
of silence. And in the stillness of the hand
that listens, a last smoke clinging to its ash.

Ringtone

As they loaded the dead onto the gurneys
to wheel them from the university halls,
who could have predicted the startled chirping
in those pockets, the invisible bells
and tiny metal music of the phones,
in each the cheer of a voiceless song.
Pop mostly, Timberlake, Shakira, tunes
never more various now, more young,
shibboleths of what a student hears,
what chimes the dark doorway to the parent
on the line. Who could have answered there
in proxy for the dead, received the panic
with grace, however artless, a live bird
gone still at the meeting of the strangers.

A Diet of Angels

So little to go on. The blade in the fan,
the warm sour air, my mother's limbs
as light as a puppet's. So few signs

but the vital ones, the final measures
of morphine and oxygen—*a diet of angels*,
we say, laughing oddly, softly, careful

with our grief as though it were sleeping.
To see her damaged look of awe, that look
of singing to someone in the distance

grown small, her voice erased in the labor
of her breathing. No more, say the leaves.
No life to waste on the gathering of life.

Then her eyes open thinly in the half dark,
and I fit her glasses over the sunken hazel,
those twin wells glazed in the last of her

body's water. Never so starless, so still.
I hold my head above them like a lamp.
The next life. What can I say of things

that frighten speech into hope or hiding.
What news do I bring to the open mouth.
She moans a bit, and we check the clock.

Soon. The crystal of her next narcotic.
Soon the dropper and its pinch of seed
so quick to flower, bitter under the tongue.

The smaller she gets, the stronger the temple
welling up with inaudible music.
Just yesterday she was calling to the dead.

Who's there, she said, *Who*—the faint survival
of her fluster going soft, mute, leading her
to a door at her bedside, the door that was not there.

All homes are her home. The one she left.
And now the shrinking of the room inside
the room. *Be well,* I say, my hand in the white

fire of her hair. Somewhere is a word
to bury the words between us. Somewhere near.
And the map of the world looks on, rough

with wear, its scattering of bright pins
for the cities she's been to, their tiny names
flowing into harbors. Each continent

is an island here. Each view a god's.
Each ship invisible. And a blue, the fallen
color of the sky, to keep the shores apart.

Elegy

Once I swore grief was the same distance
from lament as joy from praise, the same
that stretched a pillow's wing at night, a space
I'd never close completely, I'd never lose.

You know the feeling, I'm sure: the hymn
that tends the fire inside it, that keeps it safe.
But if songs are bridges to a world in flames,
don't bridges too catch fire. I want to believe

there is more pleasure in songs of loss
than loss in any song that pleases. But then
who could lose oneself inside a song
that never dies. One day our grieving turns

to lament the way a widow turns to her
remaining child. Is happiness any less
the widow, any less the mother who sees
herself in the one she prays she won't

survive. One day a mother's elegy turns
back to joy to say, don't I know you.
Another life, perhaps. Another sun
burns its arc in the slow zero of praise

we live inside, the one that lives, keeping
its vital distance. Perhaps we see praise
in the inconsolable eyes of the living.
Seeing itself is distance. And what is praise

without seeing. What are songs without
a shape that silence gives them. See that cat
who knows less of praise than the joy
that knows no joy. I love that cat. See

the birds who, or so the songs imagine,
lament our laments, though we know
better, seeing and not seeing. Like nothing
the zeroes of these eyes, these wings.

Homage to the Ear

Before words, before hunger took the shape
of words, the many shapes of chaos inside
the language of the others; before the slap

that broke us when first we spit the world
to clear our lungs, you were in there somewhere.
You were the eye to lead the eye that hid

in ways you couldn't, save inside the core
of sleep, your only silence. Though even then
you were the one dim lamp in the corner

of our house, far from the dark distraction
that consumed us. And now, look at you.
Harp of the Flesh, the way you take us down

the underworld of what we cannot know.
With every music another corridor
not unlike your own, your passage through

the body to the tiny bone of the stirrup
that goads us, wakes us; to the small hammer
that animates its anvil with a whisper.

And beyond that the water creature
of the deepest regions, our labyrinth
to keep our balance, our xylophone of hair

inside the cochlea that curls its length
into a tight spin, a final question.
Go ahead and ask. Hear the quiet strength

of your language rising, its curved song
of uncertainty, the swing of its door.
Or the way beneath our hands the ocean

in you seems to draw a little closer.
The more still we are the stronger the hush
that falls, that breaks against the warm enclosure.

Our first sound, you like to think, this wash
of air going through, though in the womb
it was your mother's breath, and you the fish

beneath the tide. Who were you to come
into this strange land you could not know
as strange, to listen locked inside the tomb

of life. What was once a mother's breath grows
into your own, more alien now than ever.
You are the rumpled sail of a ship that goes

nowhere, that lies deep inside its harbor,
awaiting the lure of some gulf stream
drawn beneath the keel, some wind to bear

you out of solitude, a constant drum
of blood, of surf, to take you from the cove
that is yours alone, and give the wind a name.

FROM *The Visible*
(2012)

Memoirs of the Five Senses

Call them the fingers of an unseen hand
that grips the world, or what we call the world,
laid here before the eye, before it welled
with light inside the tower of its well,
as if seeing crossed the dark threshold

between what we know and do not know.
Believing, we call it, however skeptical
its reputation, however soft the call
of day against the curtain's waterfall
we part to see the newly fallen snow.

The ear too takes, and in its taking tells
us something of our longing. All the time
we sleep, we hear it still: the tiny stem
of sound that descends the flower, the stream
that turns the steady chirping of the wheel.

Where there is a shell, there is an ocean,
a thing so vast we dare not call it a thing,
a great wave, or the buried lingering
as if shells were just dead enough to sing
a whispered language of the word's erosion.

And what could be more quietly alive
than the nose, the throne of intuition,
our gateway to the labyrinth. It shuns
the foul, expands the violet, lifts a fin
of flesh to lead us downward in its dive.

Quick to rouse, impossible to master,
as the kitchens of the world around it
boil and burn, and the sharp black scent
of bacon waters the tongue. Heaven-bent,
it is the watchman of what tongues remember.

If the nose is the vesper bell above,
then taste becomes the earth of its foundation.
It consecrates what the smell begins,
that writhing, that spit, that worm again
going nowhere in its teeth, its grove,

its little cemetery of nameless stones.
For some it takes a prayer to open up
the meal. For the few no holy cup
is pure enough. No mouth of theirs gapes
to melt away the wafer like a sin.

For the few it is better not to touch,
to cross the breathing boundary with a boundary,
in the womb of things that share our blood.
We wear our skin as if it were a creed.
Feeling too is believing. However much

we grasp, however closely woven the will,
we can't be sure, haunted by the slits
between our fingers, by how a body lives
in the untouched dark, this place that lifts
our gods, the shining world outside the world.

Empire of Light
after René Magritte

It's the lantern that we look to most,
there in the shape of a man with his dark hat
and radiant head, his arms cut short,
his face to the house that has no door,
or none we see, save the one the light
creates, as if the lamp were at the threshold
of its own design, however blind,
having walked this far in its sleep, alone.
It casts its blush against the closed eyes
of the shutters, against the gap between
their shades where the color warms
with the same soft fire we see in one
room still awake, in the distant corner
where someone lives or not, impossible
to tell, where some figment of our making
reads beneath a lamplight of her own.
The somnambulist knows what it is
to walk where it is neither day nor night
but both at once, as in the black tower
of these branches against the lullaby
blue of broad day, a sky-light that has no
answer in the mirror of the lake below.
The only fire there is the blurred coals
of window and lamp, the inverted
figure of our sleeper who lies face down
in the clash of ember against water.
To be both awake and asleep, is this
not one version of the afterlife,
trailed as we are by our own reflection,
to knock on the door that is no door,
and through the force of our own light, to enter.

Blaze

God knows all that wrinkled in the fire
    that night my house burned down,
what it was I felt beneath the tower
    of light, there where it crowned
everything I owned or thought I owned.
    I recall the murmur
and awe of other kids who left their homes
    to see the brilliant flutter
of sky, as if it were God's sword returned
    to take back what He gave.
The moths of ash floated on the wind,
    and I thought of the blaze
of crematoriums, how my absent father
    managed as he blessed
his father's ashes that same day, somewhere
    in a chapel to the east.
I thought of how he must have held
    a book of prayer and lowered
his eyes like a child into a well
    where everything echoed.
I always dreamed the dead hover above
    our suffering like smoke,
that they watch the blunders of our lives,
    careful as they make
their notes, as if this were the last labor
    surviving life, the hell
and heaven of it, to join in the horror
    and tedium of angels.
Just like a boy to make a mythology
    of self, to take the fear
of burning and wear it as a name, to be
    that angel in the fire.
I never saw my father weep: whoever
    did, I'll always wonder.
Perhaps it was his gift to us, to never
    snuff the northern star.

Or his grief was some nocturnal cloud
    indistinguishable
from the dark around us. It's all a closed
    chapter now, a bell
without its clapper, a night without its sleep.
    What I do know is this:
once a boy stood in his PJ's in the street,
    breathing into his fist,
feeling old among the neighbor children,
    as if it were the same
with men, however strong, the way they mourn
    not with tears, it seems,
but with a nearly inconsolable stare,
    a sense of light from
the towers of their lives, their shadows flaring,
    breaking into flame.

My Mother's Closet

After the burial, when we broke down
the estate into child's portions, to each
a broom, a ledger, the shuffle and design
of things we carried out onto the porch,

I opened what was once a closet full
of music, the vinyl now long displaced
by books, sixty or more, each a medical
companion, a difficult friend, page after page

flagged with the ragged slips of paper.
The stuff of faith, dire gospels, scores
of hymns with just one note, over and over,
just one note and a thousand horrors.

Doubtless they would argue in secret,
these pages soiled at the corners, the mind's
terrific passages shocked with highlight,
glossed with scratches in a mother's hand.

They made her the scholar of herself,
not of what she was, but of what she
could be, what she feared before the shelf
with its little study lamp, her body

glowing, lost to hours of waking sleep.
So dim, her books, she saw no end, only
the long dark well of questions, however deep
she bowed her head, anxious to believe.

People

In the land of *People Magazine,* Tara Reid
    is having a hard day.
It's her body again: too fat, too thin, too much
    of a body to fit
into our imago of the prurient angel,
    perpetually young.

Here and there the combustible cameras go on
    and off like fireflies
that hover in the dark wood. You see them burn inside
    the startle of her gaze.
I want to say, get a life, but then it is me who is
    reading *People Magazine.*

So many aging starlets, so many bright white shores
    littered with the exiles
of heaven, with the desert palms and lemon trees
    that bend with ripened fruit.
I look up from the page, and it's my turn in the chair
    at the dentist's office,

my brain gone gray as the tooth I came with, the large one
    she scrapes like a skeptic
at a hieroglyphic. It's nothing, not yet,
    she says, only the seed
of the filling shining through. And then there's the root
    of another one, exposed,

the way Tara was that night her breast slipped
    out of her drunken joy,
drunken, yes, but joy. Were this the heart of April
    I might hardly notice
the cobalt blue of morning. Halleluiah, say
    the barren limbs that point

every way but down. Tara Reid, Tara Reid,
      chirp the dusty sparrows.
And who would shame the shameless of their joy. It makes us
      feel like gods again.
The deeper our indulgence the more we turn the smooth
      complexion of the pages.

Why pair the lives of stars until their bodies collide
      with insomnia and pills,
with all the bright white teeth of sexual revenge.
      The gods know a good
disaster when they see one, the kind that scandalizes
      a goddess, that roots her

to the common ground. So it is when the divine
      mingle with blood and boredom.
They too need a story to keep the cameras
      fluttering their eyes.
Another Tara sits at her dresser brushing
      a bee from the lip

of her wine. She suffers the silences of rooms
      inside of rooms, like us.
Another god's seed enters the human the way we
      in turn enter theaters,
the way the mind enters the hole at the end of a life.
      Only a dark like this

knows what it is to turn gray and fester, to bear
      the beam of hope we shed,
not far, but far enough. One story bleeds into
      another. Cut. A wrap.
And she exits the scene, taking with her a bottle
      of something disgraceful,

something we cannot see, no one does, not now,
    not ever. She opens
her mouth; we open. Some silences are so
    thick they touch everything
like the air that touches the objects in a room.
    Something kisses her lips.

She swallows; we swallow. And then she turns away
    taking with her the need
for some last privacy and exposure all
    at once. If not youth
then abandon. If not wisdom then mystery
    which is a kind of youth.

The common birds sing their December music.
    They sprinkle the sound like water
from the hand of a priest, in fear, in joy, or both
    at once—who are you
to know, they say, and no one answers, who are you,
    they sing and will not stop.

Privacy

Forgive the older boy whose show of kindness
led me to his basement, who bent my knees
as if in prayer, the kind he used to bless

himself and things I could not speak of until
now, though I recall the thick white smell,
the musk, the mold, the salt. I taste it still,

longing for the words to take its place.
And yet I did not feel the full privacy
of shame until he held me to my silence,

which is to say I caught a glimpse of his,
how he suffered what obsession has
that cuts the actor from the act, his bliss

from my confusion. Even now surprise
looks back in the fear or guilt that froze
in him. What did I know of the difference.

Or why he turned on me, a sudden stranger,
and I an empty hall, a mirror's mirror,
and no less strange, this body now a mere

drug, a prick, a stem without the flower.
Whatever flattery I may have felt
crumbled, degenerate as a wall of flies.

Perhaps I hide my private parts away
by keeping my silence. And yet silence wakes
the sleeping man inside his sleep. It preys

on the child he is, the one who fades
into the flesh he hardly knows, his blind
compulsion red and rising. Like a blade.

Play

In my sleep there is no sleep: just me
inside a play. Not a large part, but one
with a little meat on it, with the style
of foolishness that puts you in black tights,
soft shoes, and a hat starred with a bell.
I wear my ridicule on the bus ride home,
too tired to care, I think, or know I care,
so when my body arrives, wordless, beat,
I feel heavy as a tomb in a bag of silk.

How the hell will I manage time, my skull
a costume room full of old productions.
And then the intruders: two men, two guns.
Who's to say what part of me is worthy,
why they batter the door I never lock.
So I point my pretend gun right back.
A joke. They know. I know. They wave the fingers
of their pistols as if some game were over.
But mine is better. I tell myself that.

For yours kills people, I say, and mine keeps
them alive. And even in the thick of it,
it all seems beyond belief. So what
does that make these guns. Just more props
to load, a chamber of blanks, a boy a girl
sketches in the dirt. Perhaps I should quit
this play. Such a crowded room I live in.
Such exits and entrances into the world
of work until even my sleep is work.

And God knows I need my sleep, a child's
sleep, full of the squirt guns that put tears
on the jester. Even the blindest sleep
is good, the outer space where the body
repairs itself, where the dead rise up

just before the curtain. Somewhere the scant
rain of first applause. The king is dead,
long live the king. What is a tear now
but a grain of salt, though real salt, mind you.

And what is sleep, real sleep, but the hose
we point at one another like guns inside
a summer day. Inside your crowded room,
a tiny door to the backstage dark.
The makeup bleeds flesh tones on your collar.
The heart quickens in the corpse. And rare nights
it's good to be dead, to be dead and alive
at the same time. To be somewhere between
the acts, between the salt of sleep and that

of work, between guns that don't work and those
that do, granted, as something to get us safely
through our story. It is good to be dead,
to be in the arms of the father who carries
his sleeping child from the playhouse to the car.
How large the oldest theaters of being
foolish, of the droopy silk and bell
on the long ride home, through hushed amusement,
the fade to black, deeper into the silent cheer.

Milk

Ask any star, flame to flame, any infant
mouth that tugs the long and twisted rope
of light, that pulls a tether to the world.

We drink and so ignite the word for what
we drink, what consumes us in its music.
The mere mention is its own erasure.

And soon it arrives, this breakfast table,
these words we lay against our tongues like forks.
The pitcher tilts. The fire flashes as it braids.

We think *of* and *about,* and so the bridge
and the barrier of how we think,
the want that sets our thinking into motion.

When our mother tongue was just a child,
desire too fell from the night sky,
from the stars, says the book of tongues.

And since the brain was one enormous cloud
that came between us and the universe
we would conceive, one was never here there.

Stars looked down their rifles in the fog.
All we want would kill us, surely, our eyes
awash in the blood of the human heart.

And yet to want to be wanted, to flee
our skin like music from a radio,
it speaks of certain liberties, yours, mine.

Where there is power, there is no love.
I read that once. Can it also be true
how strong the solitude that overpowers

its own illusion, our breath repeating against
the shore. A surge peaks above the child
before it buckles beneath its weight, and gives.

To give, to relent, to wake each time
to a heart so quick you swear it isn't yours.
Which is to say you can, in some measure,

long for what you have, as if the trembling
of one body broke you into two.
Take the man who walks the streets at night

to remind himself, yes, he has arms, legs,
that he wants these things, that he moves
forever toward his lifetime in the distance.

Men like that talk to themselves. They wonder
aloud for the company of strangers,
unsure what it was that snipped the braid,

the face of sleep descending like an anchor.
Those who never dream are always dreaming.
The earth tilts. The clouds spill from north to south.

That sound you hear. Where would you put it.
Where to lay our heads like some luminous
breakfast at the end of our journey.

When, I ask, will the moment linger
long enough to share this meal, to talk
of the departed with a distant music

in its voice. Does it create suffering,
the light we drink to mend our suffering. I know
I talk to no one when I ask the dead.

Behind these leaves are holes the shapes of leaves.
I hear them crackle in the trees like milk.
Still I keep returning to my friends

swallowed up in that surge of fire.
Come out, night replies, and so the names
come spilling over in a trickle of jewels.

No star is one word I use for all the stars.
Come out, says the sky to the planet,
says friend to friend, mother to the dire

thirst that eyes the sister stars of nipples,
that puts its mouth to the future and so
draws the great white silk, as if to drain

the lamp that way, to dim the source that is
this cloud, this breast, this small ghost voice
as it darkly whispers, *there there, there there.*

FROM *Choir of the Wells: A Tetralogy*
(2013)

Ink

When, in the dark ages of the East,
the Mongols took the heart of the city
and poured in, room after room, to cut
a path through the bodies in their way,
they loaded up the illuminated books,
the many wildflowers of Islam hand-sewn,
penned, edged in gold, and made of them
a bridge across the Tigris, shaky at best,
to lead men from the spoils of their labor.
This is the story of the House of Wisdom,
how centuries gathered there to pool
the gems of medicine and metaphysics,
until the river took them, leaving us
the ache of knowing just enough to ache.
If history repeats, it does so without us.
It returns the way a criminal returns,
or a tongue to the space that was a tooth.
When the bodies of the philosophers
broke the surface, they floated here and there,
littering the shore, their wounds drained
into the current, to stain the glass
not red exactly, in spite of what you hear,
but rust, a fading scar of dirt and iron.
The greatness of a city is how it kneels
near the water, to beat its laundry there,
or flood the fields in their season, to carry
what: fennel, flax, cinnamon, a scholar.
Beyond the necessary, a river draws
the mourner toward something she cannot find—
it helps her nonetheless—or the believer
toward reconciliation with her god.
If we hear there rumors of water going
on without end, it is nonetheless loss
that speaks. What book would not be a bridge.
Or the grave of some sad misconception.
Somewhere still there is a volume that says

what the river of the dead cannot,
that once a library fell into the Tigris,
and these waters, that are a widow's friend,
ran black with ink, mile after mile.

The Invisible Hand

> Our life has no end the way our visual field has no limits.
> —LUDWIG WITTGENSTEIN

Light, we know, is an invisible thing.
The beam that falls through the theaters
of a childhood—we trust it's there

thanks only to the dust that floats inside it,
and the screen, of course, the stuff that takes
the dark of light and makes of it a story.

In this way light provides a language
for the dawn of things, ourselves, for instance,
how we travel through the first two years

into the luminous amnesia of who
we are, blind to the gods of days that made us.
A body might be replaced twelve,

thirteen times over, every cell hung
on the architecture of what goes missing,
the way the widow hangs on her son's arm,

on the strength inside his long black sleeve.
Today I listened to Ravel's *Concerto*
for the Left Hand, to its vague beginnings

in the bass violins, the rocking cradle
of the bow as if it were tuning up
for what's to come, for the slow emergence

of a subject, the polish of the brass,
the great wave that peaks and washes ashore
the hand, the A, the lowest of the keys.

It's the announcement of our soloist
whose body lies buried in the ghost
of sound. Do you think of him as well,

Paul Wittgenstein, the man who lost his arm
to a Russian bullet, how he woke
in a prison hospital to find it gone.

He could not see this yet as the birth
of all the left-hand scores he would commission,
Ravel's, for one. In truth, music's origins

are the casualties of every age.
Given time days wept a pool of light
over charcoal keys he sketched on a crate.

And as he taught his hand to play the parts
that were not there, the reach of it grew
desperate, quick, as if it were two hands,

worlds apart, one dead, another living,
each one abandoned by the other,
bound by that to the talk between them.

What is more intangible than the past
to come. Remember, him on stage, the tuck
of the sleeve that fluttered in its pins.

I have seen his performance in a movie,
his hand leaping like a bird on fire,
as if all he lost brought on an excess

of life. The madness and the suicides
of a tragic family—they can break you
down or open, or a little of both.

You can almost hear him as he turns
to his brother to say, is it true,
what we cannot speak about we must

pass over in silence. But what if
silence too begins to speak, or sing,
to be the hand that is no longer there.

What if death is dark as any beam
that illuminates a score of music.
Birth too. Or the want to give birth

and so be born. There is no idea
as powerful as the will to have one.
And as the orchestra gathers up

its strength beneath the hand, everything
falls the way a building falls through
blooms of dust. I live for times like that,

for beginnings, ends, the great dark hall
alive and listening, the light we only
know as light the moment that it's broken.

Benthos

The fathoms take what we know of light,
the ache of it that dims as it goes
cold, deeper into the ache of dark.

Down here an eye is its own lantern,
sunk among the cuttlefish and squid,
the angel flesh that swims among the wreckage.

Today I walked into a small museum.
On a wall, a hill of spectacles,
teeth, a memoir bound in human skin.

I have read this book, skin to skin,
and yet I think a part of me reads it
in the dark. If this is the past,

it is far too tiny and too enormous.
What you make out in the many faces
gets lost in the unspeakable focus

of one. And each one difficult to name,
to recognize now, beneath the mask
of no mask. Not enough food to live,

and too much to die. That's what they say.
And it goes on that way for a while,
until the story of the boy who begs

to be shot. The core of us is strange.
Bones of faces float to the surface.
And deeper still, a voice, neither theirs

nor ours. Like a heavy net of cautions
that binds us to a world. Perhaps a prayer,
a memoir's future tense, or the last

breath of a man, here, high above the dark
floor, above the drowned, as we know them,
the gas blue eel, our black and silent stars.

Pill

Say you are high all the time save those moments
you take a sobriety tablet and so descend
the nerves of the heart, thinking straight,

they call it, as if the mind were an arrow
shot from the eye into the eyes of others,
the ones you wronged, the ones you never knew

you love or do not love, the black fathoms
of their pupils deepening as your eyes close.
And sure it hurts, how something dead walks out

your sleep, how it goes from blue to red
like blood. And yet the stuff keeps calling you
in a father's voice. You loved your father,

so it's more than bitter seeds you swallow.
It's quiet pleasure within the limitations
of one life, until the great space of a day

gets wider, brighter, as if you were slipping
into summer with its giant measures
of desire, the way just sitting makes it rise.

And yes, with each dose comes the gravity
and boredom, the slow crush of August heat,
though you are learning to live here, in a town

with one good street to speak of, one flock of trees
to storm the night. In time you are addicted.
And it takes more of the drug to get you back

to the world, where morning swallows flit
in last night's rain. In time you tell yourself
you are the age you are: the little pains

inside your arms, your legs, they are just that:
the pinch that says you are not asleep,
that the compulsion you feel is the pull

of the planet you walk, alone. And the dawn,
however deep you breathe, is everyone's now,
everyone's breath in the sky above you,

everyone's sun aching into layers
of mist, spitting fire in the eye,
its one black star dissolving, like a pill.

My Death Space Dot Com

Now that obituaries come online
with coroner reports and full disclosure,
imagine the ways to betray a man
come out of hiding to die. Ask the bloggers
who weigh in on my friend's bad habit,
who make of it their own drug strung out
across a mirror, so when they pay tribute
to their power, how they had their doubts
about his talent, his flu, I think how lucky
I was to receive the kindness of the weak.
My death space, as they call it, as if it's me
who died. A life, we know, is complex.
But death is simple. A place to talk shit,
to license grief, or barring that, to kill it.

Robitussin

The boy who stood, patient, alone,
outside my night class in the cold,
who waited out the hangers-on
who held me with their final questions,
or shyly handed me their drafts,
the waver of their long hand.
The boy who watched the others
step against their cigarettes and break
their conversations, him there
half-hidden by the trees, hands
in pockets as if to clutch a coin in each.
The boy who followed me stair
by stair to the dim confessional
that was my office, walled in the faces
of friends and teachers, long dead,
with eyes to read what I read in them.
We were just a bunch of lonely boys,
he said. And then the furtive
details, the four bottles a night,
the syrup in his bones, how the high
was a bit like codeine at first,
then turned visionary, dire. Weird,
he said, and then again, having arrived
at that place where words sink
back into the throat that made them.
And I saw him on some gated dock
in Houston, gazing through the empty
bottle at the light of a ship
in the distance. He had that pallor
that was half-alive, half-angelic,
and that glass heart of the addict,
the sense he saw something in that ship
neither approaching nor drifting off,
just a bobbing in the malaise that was
the waters of the bay. Lonely boys,

he called them, the dispossessed
who slipped their vial of shame
and excitement from a bag,
their pupils wide with the night's
great and empty spaces. What
do you say to a boy whose head
bows at land's end, that it's true,
that suffering teaches nothing,
not mere suffering, suffering alone,
however far it hopes to take you
past the sour dumpsters
through the shooting galleries
of harbor towns moaning like ships.
Not the gulf refineries that puzzle
the sky, the way the floodlight
on their bones guides a vandal
through the fences, through eyes
that only a child can thread.
Some boys are boys forever
staring out at the black tanker
carving forward, sluggish and deep,
the rainbow of the engine's
water streaming out for miles.
Not suffering alone, but the long
negotiation of days to follow.
Which is why he was there
after all, the boy in my office.
Surely there is virtue in the invitation,
in the word that hallucinates
the child who fell asleep
with a ruby of poison by his heart.
Imagine the flash of the prow
that cuts the mind like bread,
that says, this is my body. Come.
Eat. Eat and be whole again.

Drink until your feet dangle off
the edge of the landing and walk.
A ship named *Lost* chafes
at its anchor. A searchlight dims.
Gods lean down in their bodies
made of emptiness and fire:
tomorrow, tomorrow. Tonight
I am grateful to the language
that elevates a boy stair by stair,
to the inexpressible that begins
the journey. I am grateful
to the flesh that dissolves
into words which in turn long
for the flesh once more, the stranger
a child curls inward to comfort,
to survive, to carry home, to be there
in the end, no child at last,
no harbor friend beside him as he wakes.

Homage to Sebastian Stenzel

After the cedar died in the great fire,
it stood for eighty years. A testament
to what the long neglected can endure
if the roots go deep, the heartwood dense,
grain woven, limbs upholding nothing
like a nervous system of the sky.

No need to clear the lion's share of damage,
the land the blaze blackened for a season,
though naturally they razed the crumpled home.
What the fire began, men completed,
and there were those who were buried here
and there, and those who never reappeared.

What remained was the flame of soot
that climbed the tower, our useless miracle,
guardian of those who stood in its shadows
and suffered without record, passing through
the stories and nightmares of a few
friends, neighbors, until they too passed on.

Nights, the long and stubborn musculature
swung its axe in the wind, laying low
a silence in the branches, and in the stars
that slept there, that burned for eighty years.
It took a luthier to bring them down,
to see in the tone-wood a slow growth

the winters made stiff and tight, ideal
in its resistance and yield, its open voice.
So yes, he destroyed it, quarter sawn so
the monument might fall again, and again,
over and over as song in the startled
braces of the instrument. Or so he hoped.

It takes a little faith to flex the final
cut, to tap it listening for some pitch
to draw breath in the unspoken, to say
I am out there somewhere, as music is
in the reticence of things. It takes
an ember's patience to plane the wood just so,

to fit it over the casket, over the memory
of one note dying into the next,
into some solitary conversation,
the still bodies of those who listen, those
who, for the moment they are listening,
stand in the fire, made tall, and have no name.

The Blindness of Needles
after Goya

When a maker of images goes deaf,
he sees a world clarified by silence,
a lens wept over the things unspoken.
Doubtless this is why we find the man
facedown on a drawing table, hands
on his head to shelter him from flocks
that feast on sleep. The blood in his hair,
the lynx, the bats, more than beast, less
than human, all dark fuel for the lantern.
The etcher's needle shines as it cuts.
It takes enormous care, to draw the curve
of a manacle, to rust it shut,
not with neglect, but with the precision
of a scar. Night sweeps the avenues
into brothels, asylums. These sure proportions,
they give to nightmare a logic, an edge
to deepen the line where the acid pours.
Across the cobblestones of Madrid,
lamps beat the laundry of their shadows.
The hearts of the city loosen their fists.
If reason sleeps, as the etching says,
it dreams. Like any theater, the blacker
the wings, the more fiercely we believe.

The Unfinished Slave

The man we see writhing in the marble,
what is he without the strength of all
we do not see. A slave, we are told,
though to what: the rock, the king, the world
that, cut or uncut, we can't remember.
To be distinct, chiseled as a number
across a grave, that was his dream once.
If only he could shake the rough stone
from his back, instead of being one.
Or if he stood naked before the tomb
he was meant to guard, perhaps then
he would wear a god's glass complexion.
As is, he is abstract, and so closer
to us, to the life that makes a future
the anticipated past, our heads half
buried, blind, disfigured by the stuff
to which we owe our restlessness, our art.
The hand that carves its figure in the slate
abandons it, thinking it will lie
beneath its work some day, beneath a sky
that refuses to commit, to lift.
It's in there somewhere, whatever's left
of those who drive a hammer into us.
With every blow, a little bloom of dust
flies. Time keeps its promise to itself.

Elegy for the Spanish Republic

> No rendering of the appearance of reality can move us
> like a revelation of its structure.
> —ROBERT MOTHERWELL

On the other hand there is the body
whose skin draws so tight about the bones
it makes plain the shield across the heart,
which is to say, the decay of anyone,
of nations no less, coaxes to the surface
something bold, impoverished, the infrastructure
that wears our nervous system like a coat.

In a photo made abstract by time,
a soldier props his rifle on the great swell
of a dead horse, finding protection there,
where all flesh is gray, the black salt
of the emulsion eroded by the light.
Death simplifies. Resolves. It pins
one fear to the other in its crosshairs.

Despotic, you could say, though it opens
up a man's gaze, as if in looking hard,
here behind the guardian smoke of homes
on fire, he saw his own cry approaching.
Every soldier is a metaphysician
who sends a bullet through the skin to see
there the deeper workings of a regime.

It takes a workman's brush in the fist
to paint the great bars of a testament
to silence, to the sheer scale of it drawn
over the mouths of those who weigh down
the wagons in the street. Are they jailed there,
these open sores on the canvas, these eyes,
or do they wet the stiffening insistence

of the lines, the arced exclamations,
writ large, bent against the quiet tide.
White, from lead mostly, highly toxic.
Black, from charred bones, horns, even gas.
Together they make a language indelible,
scarred, and yet, it is the gesture we see,
the assertion of a widow's love hurled

at the speed of rage. We do not look
the way we feel, at once enormous and small,
as if we were both the iconography
and its citizen, its eye. A thing, perhaps,
but so too the flash that is the x-ray
of our grief, that strikes a blow in stillness
where the plow of the sternum begins to rise.

Limestone

Our law was built to withstand the wind,
here where spring is no paradise, strong
against the courthouse tower, our stones bound
in grit, chiseled thick as an arm is long.

And at the entrance a Confederate
soldier, a boy—he too is chiseled—his face
a tomb of old confusions, of nights
he woke, panicked by his father's voice.

Mostly he goes unnoticed, oblivious
in turn, where the hammers rise and fall
against the criminal. The last bar closes.
Some child writes his hatred on the wall.

It's everywhere and nowhere, like blood.
Or nails no nation sinks beneath its gavel.
Only time. The other fatherhood.
Stones without the conscience to be cruel.

Audubon

1

The night my father died I buried myself
in a little language, a testament of will,
measured out the way the stonecutter

measures out our names to make them fit,
and as I leaned beneath the bell of light
to the cursor where it pulsed, I placed there

neither man nor the shape of his absence,
not grief as I knew it, but the tiny bones
of ink that grief made, rising to the surface.

I have met with those who disapprove
of passing through too quickly into song,
as if, with death, we give to it the first

word which is none at all. Anything more
is to make light of suffering: mine, yours.
Or worse, to make far too much of it,

to lose oneself in the futures market
that seeks to clear a profit on misfortune.
They have a point. That is, some songs need

a certain hesitation to break the ice
and move more deeply into winter's current.
Then again, tending to a song's needs

gives loss a vocation, and who is to say
what will come of it, any more
than what comes of music while it lasts.

2

Audubon loved the creatures that he killed.
That is part of the story. He loved the music
he silenced, gutted, stuffed with clouds of cotton,

the bodies he cleansed with a surgeon's care
then mended with needle, a stitched seam
tucked beneath the feathers where they shone.

He loved the eyes that gave way to seeds
of glass, the small black blisters gleaming
with light that went just so far, so deep.

Somewhere in that region of inquiry,
in what he could not paint, the illusion
of life took, and fluttered to the surface,

informing the angle of the head, the beak,
the bright rustle of wings as the ivory-
billed woodpecker turns away from us

to make out some motion in the distance.
Movement is danger. Or so the heartbeat
says at first, until it settles back

onto its perch, its branch of understanding.
What you see within the sure lines and blush
of these renditions is an artist's gaze,

so steady, cautious as it crosses the lip
of stillness, our open coffin, careful not
to break the perfect silence where it breathes.

3

Suppose all the world is a house lit up
against the night, and the eye of the bird
our only window. If you look through

the black air, you just might see a man,
a father, say, who takes his broken sleep
down the hall to a desk in the distance.

He is peering over his heavy glasses
to the near at hand, papers that await
his signature to put his affairs in order.

When he writes, his pen bleeds a little
ink over the line, real or imagined,
to lay a name against the emptiness.

Birds slip into the flowered portraits
of his study, silent, and yet made flesh
by the hand that murdered to create them.

The Carolina pigeon dips the nib
of his beak into the mouth he feeds.
If he spreads his colors, ribbed in black,

it is one more song that calls the thing
unseen. The man closes up his desk,
and with it a passage in his testament,

the part where he asks to be scattered,
remembered the way a body remembers to breathe.
A ghost thread pulls outward, like a word.

The Lost Year

After the storm, when the wind pulled down
all that was high and dying from the trees,
when the north blew out the candle of our home,
our roof chipped, gutters flooded, it seemed
so unlikely, the calm that followed, the strength
of blue, the kind of quiet a room possesses
after a banquet. Clouds passed like ships on fire.

And I thought of the lost year, the one
of the gaping summer, the tentative one
that opened up your body like a question.
Tell me if you can. What has the flesh taught you
in its difficult season. There are days,
no doubt, that turn away the gift of knowledge
like a parcel with a clock inside.

Still you must admit. The road feels more
spacious now, though more solitary,
more uncertain. Stars gem the damaged branches.
They clarify the gaps between. These nights
you tug a little darkness to your chin.
But then, what do I know. Only the space
of not knowing, how near it is and always.

You dip your spoon into a bowl of milk
to row across the white pool.
You of all people understand
the blessings of appetite. You gape, you swallow,
and the world keeps moving through you.
It is the wind in the torch, the blood in the muscle.
Go on, it says. Even without knowing
now, you die a little into joy.

Homage to Phosphorus

Phos, light, *pherein,* to bear, and bear it
we must, as the compounds of the brain
will tell you, there is no thought without it.

True, there are horrors in this story,
the napalm that drenched the boy who ran barefoot
toward the camera, his arms opened slightly

so as not to sting himself with himself.
And before that, the bones of women
brittle with the stuff it took to work

the match factories of the past. Proof.
The molecules of fire will kill you.
Which is more than the man could know,

the alchemist who stumbled on it first
in his search for the philosopher's stone,
his hands scarred with alkalai and acid.

His eyes poor, head bowed, he raised a puzzle
of glass to corrupt things and so make them
pure, to steam the urine in his flask.

Which is when a snow began to fall
like nights we are sleeping and the dust
that burns white with cold gathers below.

As a boy I owned a toy moon that glowed
with something toxic on the one side,
and I inhaled its sulfurous smell, thinking

I, too, would drink the shine of the place
and give it back to darkness. In reality
phosphorescence was no mirror, no moon,

but a furnace that consumes the air.
Those were the years of the rain and war
in southeast Asia. I barely understood it,

even though the cameras offered us
the parts a nation could not take, and did.
Somewhere great blooms of phosphorus fell

from crop dusters and crinkled through the vines.
Mostly those who volunteered were boys.
And neither old nor brave enough, I killed

my toys of them, green beneath a moon
that had two sides, one dead, the other deadly.
One disaster led to another, to the cross-

hair flash that was death from a distance.
The new wars look less and less like wars.
Just a snow of little conflagrations

that break against the desert sand at night.
History repeats nothing, say the lights.
It burns a map across the child, a country

that spreads into an empire I do not know
as mine. It burns the way gold burns,
or the sun that would liquefy our gold,

or the sickness that lingers long after
some difficult fact, some news, say,
made strange and personal by a soldier

at the door in dress blues; one word and she
who receives it suddenly a widow,
transfixed by fire, her eye wet with new light.

Luminescence of the Oceans

There is a drowned fire in our leaving.
You see it in the wakes of ships that cut
a passage through the red tide, the sparks

thrown aft as they welter in the current.
Sometimes when I look down at the seeds
of light, I keep returning to the furrow

that made a stranger of my father's body,
the way he slept beneath the surgeon's lance,
the saw, the red hand that reached inside

to turn the organ over. Sleep or no sleep,
a literal heart fumbles with the things
it cannot say and so it says again.

Look at waves. They fold into themselves
the sob of oceans, like a frightened child.
You would think they get tired of it,

how, as they heave exhausted to the bed
of sand, the last remains of day crackle
in the fall. I talk about my father

because, beyond the obvious, I am
afraid the water will swallow him again.
When I look ahead, I see something

futureless there, the jewel of the star
that drizzled into his eye that day.
It seems so still, though I know better.

The machinations of the ocean break
into the million small decisions of the deep.
It lives to move. The star that dissolves

against the foam, it goes somewhere. It must.
Beneath the widow's lace, perhaps, or here
inside the gaze that reads. It spreads its net.

FROM *For the Lost Cathedral*
(2015)

The Gate

When first I came into the world,
I wept at the sting of light
and steel that cut me as I gasped.

The black rain kindled a quiet
fire in the window, and I listened
to a distance that had no language.

That was the 50's, when Asia
slept beneath a drizzle of ash
that had been falling since the war.

When I first learned of heaven,
it was something we lost, or was
loss simply the word we gave it.

When I heard my nation's stories,
they were the words of a father
who gave me words. I was what I feared.

If there is a pearl gate up there,
I see it as a guillotine
that chooses its friends carefully.

The eye of the needle, the narrow
passage, they would straighten us.
The sound of rain would make us open.

Advent

On an island in the disputed region
of the Yellow Sea, blooms of smoke
from the shelling of the garrison
weave into one bloom, one force of nature
so thick, they say, you cannot see your hands.
The planet, we know, tilts on its axis
like a man contemplating a problem,
spun toward the horizon of another
year, always forward, across a winter
where we celebrate an advent so long
past it could have been most any season.
Islanders will tell you, the farther back
you go the more it dims into a future,
the one we carry as a grudge or gift
to lay at the threshold of a child's bed.
Nights when the cold draws its curtain
on our homes, we turn to the windows
of TV's and stare, alone with the war
and its commercials, the firestorm
that breaks a motherland in two like bread.
We too break, each year a little more
divided at heart as we cough by the fire,
still and sleepy as cows in the crèche,
thinking it is one thing for a king
to kneel, another for him to seek advice.
The modern kings do not wander far
into the desert, but tend to sit and watch
the monitors fill up with falling lights.
Facts are hard, like the man who buries
his hatchet in the turkey he shares
with a neighbor, with talk that turns bitter
as it grows more national in scope.
Say I am the offspring of the thought
I just had, flesh of its flesh, and so
different, in some measure culpable, free,

as anything alive. A child is born,
crowned in blood, and we lighten up.
Sure, we see it every day, and yet
this day, tradition says, is unlike any,
which is true. It has never happened,
and never will again, over and over
the will to be reborn, to gasp and cry
forgiveness, that is, like birth, difficult,
scared, insurgent, brave with the stranger,
the winter child, that blossoms through the wound.

Sleeper

As a boy, I took a night train over the border,
above acres of tenements and town squares

locked in the black box of winter. Go home,
said the quiet streets, just beyond the scrawl

of graffiti and electric wire that held us, bound
for West Berlin. Everywhere the unspoken

contract with a past no boy could understand,
let alone me, there, behind the passenger window,

my bleached face gone dim as the dark fell through.
Block after block the dull terror of cities

like warehouse districts alive with citizens—
they must be out there somewhere—though who was I to say.

Late came early in the heart of the regime,
or so I imagined as I slept, best I could,

the train shuddering like a waterfall around me.
In time the noise whitened to an emptiness

that drowned the inner ear, a veil over the voices
which in turn veiled the silence of the season.

There, in my sleep, I could not sleep, and so stepped
into the city, looking for a lamp in the glaze

of some chained window, a curtain to rustle,
a code to crack. Which is when I caught my own eye

in the glass, collar turned against the wind,
and asked, who am I to trust the person that I see.

December made the stars harder, their secrecy
more ruthless. What I would not give to sleep

a deeper sleep, and so I lay in the snow,
weary as an hourglass, feeling less and less,

as all the while a locomotive in the distance
plunged farther to the north, to the chamber of engines

where a boxcar from Warsaw went still, latched in horror,
and the smell of chimneys drifted through the door.

Lebensraum

When the ashes of the last great war
settled on the ramshackle factories
and chapels of the Rhine, you could hear
a concertina walk the crooked alley

to beg beneath the window for a coin
or two, for some chime from the towers
of rooms and radios that held our nation.
What we wanted was out there, beyond the scars

ships cut across the river in the distance.
So when the man at the microphone spoke
with such force his German spit at us,
we listened, as if a thunderhead broke

our wings, not down, but open, less proud
than nailed to pride's surrogate, his face
a scaffold for the angry and the wounded.
Suns fell. Music faded. And in their place,

we lay and listened for the carriage wheel,
the bell, the hinge, the banner that chirped
as it descended, as one by one we fell
like coins, to shatter all the hearts of Europe.

Cross of Nails

The morning after the blitzkrieg that toppled the vaults
of Saint Michael's Cathedral and set the rest on fire,

a stonemason found among the embers one roof
beam laid across another, a kind of crucifix

created by the forces of accident and violence
and then by grace of eyes that saw in them an order.

A puzzler of rubble and its hidden logic,
he chiseled the words *Father, forgive,* then lashed and raised

the crux into a monument, an abstract man,
beneath the gutted tower left unrepaired for good.

Forgiveness forgets nothing—any cross will tell you—
but calls as witness a common father to ask of us

what we then would ask of him. *Forgive them, Father,*
say the reddened letters in the large black book

that, some claim, is God talking to God, or a man
to men, or both at once. Oh, it gets confusing,

the dust that falls for weeks over the bombed cathedral
as the search party lays its dead in the street.

Coventry, Dresden, Berlin, they know a thing or two
about confusion, the grief that makes a home a stranger,

a stranger a home in ruins you think you understand.
You do and do not, and the things that go unsaid

are tender sometimes as wounds are and certain mothers,
certain gathering storms that call their children in.

As roofs go, so go their nails, and the oldest ones
were so long and fierce, the men of Saint Michael's

torched three into the mast-like symbol of their faith,
the vertical axis with its dagger toward the earth.

And they gave it away, shipped it across the channel.
Walk the ruins of the Kaiser Wilhelm Cathedral,

and you see there the heavy iron nails raised up
like an anchor drawn to heaven's invisible hull.

Call it confession or kindness, it is, and no less sharp
than all that makes forgiveness possible and hard.

It is specific, as givers and receivers are.
And yes, it would raise us up in turn. And yes,

it is still a nail and so longs to be struck,
immersed, remembered. Call it the drizzle of soot,

the inconsolable cry, the widows of England
facedown in their pillows. Call it what you will,

this stake in the nation, the heart, the corpus mundi,
this gift that would be yours. The moment that you give it.

Threnody
after Penderecki

In an alley where the world ends,
I have found a door. It opens
to those who have no other
home, who walk as strangers
to these streets. I see them
always, and they are strangers still.
I hear in them a threnody
that is a field of all the notes
at once, even those that fall
between the ones we know,
joined the way that flames join
the walls of smoke and molten glass.
The architecture of memory
burns a thousand different ways,
its skin drawn back, a thousand
different silences behind it.
There are stories our forgetting
makes safe enough for grief,
embers stirred the way we stir
a tin of soup, or spare change.
A record spins on its needle.
The pages that trouble me most
crumple in the heart's furnace,
in the iron that gives off heat
years after the ash resolves.
My furnace has a latch, a door,
where a hand comes and goes,
its arm far away somewhere.
It has a hinge that sings across
the threshold, a mouth that gapes
as it listens, as it disbelieves
the news buried inside the music,
at least until the music ends
and history is a heart that opens
itself, alive, and walks right through.

Idolatry

No end to the little sacraments
of the near at hand, the clock, the pen,
the watchful telephone, the many wires

of its nervous system a world wide web,
all of us bound, alone in our rooms
with one another, invisibly enormous.

If you too stare at the receiver and talk
until the face on the other line
lies buried beneath a grid of numbers,

it is no idol you see, only a passage,
an effigy inside its tablet, a night
that falls through the window as we sleep.

And yet it is tempting, as the connection
breaks, to leave you with some bad news
you have yet to hear, to look the phone

in the mouth, and continue conversation.
No idol. Just you and the thing as you
exchange your gifts, and since the telephone

draws its voice from out there somewhere,
you feel small in light of your other self
like a child before a statesman's statue.

My things give me comfort, I tell my fear
in jest, in the knowledge I will lose them.
Gods come and go, they say, but things,

they are immortal. Look at the teen idol,
not the person, but the headshot, the gloss,
the sheen that lights the pink above its bed.

It knows what it is to solar eclipse
the man who made it all possible.
And as such, it shields the curious

from certain blindness, to make visible
only the outline of the source, the crown,
a totality so like the human eye

with its black coin laid across the light.
In the desert once a tribe adorned
a gold calf who looked back through its boredom,

a cow after all, and a dead one at that,
bemused by their dance about the fire.
All that gold, why not eat the real thing.

If you had your choice, would you consume
a god, or kneel starved for power, with power,
humble as the brick that seals its palace.

The avenues of my city gleam with malls
where kids like me go to watch, to say,
yes, I live among the others, with each

a face a mirror wears like a fine shirt.
I know a man who lost his wife to divorce
and so went out to walk the tall aisles

of his K-mart, drenched in the ordinary
radiance that was a love song gone bad.
One too many light bulbs to explain it.

Everywhere the half-distracted chirping
of a music, the air-conditioned tunes
that move along, that hope for better things.

It helped to return one broken object
for another, but more, just seeing people
who once had vanished in his happiness.

No malls in the land of radio silence,
in the anchorite kingdom of the north,
where the concentration camps are small

cities far below our satellites,
our glass-bottom boats that float in disbelief.
Not things, but the monotheism

of one thing, one image everywhere,
one statue with its monumental arm.
When the blind remove their bandages

to see, it is not the surgeon they turn to
with their tears, hands raised, bodies crushed
beneath their gratitude, but their dear

leader, the general, the iconography
they fear, they love, or both, the face that burns
in theirs this image of a soldier, his coat

a people's blue that touches the flesh that is
no flesh, only a god, the common cloth
of one man a nation weeps for as it kneels.

Harvest

Must it be the spot upon the x-ray
that becomes our autumn cloud, our hole
to view the contents of our lives, to pray
into perhaps with the greed of the fragile
at heart. Must it be the broken will
that bends our knees to speak with the unknown.
Why the sickbed as our first cathedral,
or the ailing father our wafer, our wine.
Why must the well of the oracle
call back from its throat inside the earth
to make us into strangers as we kneel.
Somewhere beyond the mirror of our death,
we were light once, thrown open, ever near
to what, we could not say, blind with rain
that broke so fast against the back of summer
who thought to praise its fury as we ran.

Tallow

In de la Tour's *St. Joseph,* the carpenter
leans over the awl in his hands, his sandal
braced against the block, against the stair
that leads us up the cross of the handle,

up these arms exposed to fully realize
the strength in them, up the tourniquet
of his sleeve to the mountainous horizon
of his shoulders, his head, his silhouette

bowed with power. His body stoops to harbor
the meager candlelight his child holds,
the red translucence of the child's fingers
no less a shelter, their wild flame withheld

from us, though we see it in the father's
eye, the way he looks not at his own grip
but at the boy's, the danger there, the fire
that smokes above the glowing fingertips.

Always the missing thing to pull the old
gaze away, however slightly, displaced
by fear that bathes a child's skin in gold.
All things the orphan of some other place.

Even the candle began inside the shadow
of some barn, in the meat of the beast
that gave its life to those here, its tallow
to their room, their labor, the air they breathe.

As for the man who dipped his paintbrush
in the thickening shade—how little we know
of the nights he spent, the weary stretch
of cloth he draped across the morning window.

That he was the son of a baker, sure.
That, as he aged, his canvases took on
the bread and earth tones of what was near,
what lit the quiet of his meditation.

Whatever the history, the painting falls
silent, and so gives the eye more space
to move, bemused, free, the way the awl
moves freely inside the mark it makes.

Close your eyes and you see what strains
the back of the craftsman, the perfect posture
of a block of wood where days lie down,
get up, and down again, over and over.

You see in the unseen the need that shapes
a chair, a boy, a painter's canvas, a past
soaked in blood and oil, in light that breaks
whatever char to warm the midnight in us.

In each pupil a bead of black wax
as if sight began in dark. To better bind
man to child, the fire to its wick,
the blush of tallow to the living hand.

For the Lost Cathedral

1

One life, one life, one life, and so
the secret life, it began so shyly,
glittering the highest branches,

breaking in droplets over the rooftops,
a near mist, he thought, so quietly it came.
And though it seemed to fall

over everything, every gesture and scrap
of clothing, every word escaping
his lips, though it lengthened

its low green blades in the morning sun,
it lay forever at a distance
like the crackle of a river

becoming always something else,
the missing thing that bears the name
of the river. That bears the voice:

*To split your life into two lives, yours
and the secret's, to divide the mind,
to break your death into two deaths now,*

*as if to multiply that one last breath
so that it might shatter into two breaths,
and four, a whole flock of breaths,*

to bury yourself in the living choir.

2

There are men, he thought, who grip
the secret so hard it shrinks
to the size of a fist, incarnate,

men who light his TV at dusk,
who lay their lives at the footstool
of the secret, unable to look up,

fierce with the shame that is their goodness.
Iconography flutters on a wall
like the papered shrine of a stalker's closet.

There are men who envy
the sweethearts of martyrs,
men whose death is the bride

of the secret, who slip into a ring
of wire, ribbed in explosives,
who cry out the way a lover cries,

in abandonment, in prayer.

3

Though no one knows the truth
of the secret's birth, no one
would presume it had one

as we know it, there are tales—
like the story of the woman
downed in the booby-trapped jungle,

far from home, seeing
in her broken skin the arrival
of a force, the sheer gore

a glory, which, if not the secret,
is nevertheless its messenger,
the speed of the angel

come in a flash to fill that gap.
God, she said, cursing, *God,* again
more softly now, like a call

to no one no one intended,
not fully, just the rising
apparition on her lips, a language

pouring from the open wound.

4

What's a name, he asked,
that some would give it freely
to each thing they love save

the whole of love, this thing
that is nothing and all of it,
this wish that moves from near

to far, the very wits of near,
the very far that loves to surpass
the far. What's in a voice

as if names were ours and so the named.
Look at the names of the field
where the weather wears them.

You see a girl with a finger
in the grooves of letters.
As if names were flesh and so the named.

To put the secret anywhere
he thought less of words
than of the eye, the circled circle,

how named or nameless we enter
at a distance. Just like a circle
to love a distance, to be

both womb and portal, rose
and world, the hold of the well
and the round voice of empty space:

is there anyone there, there, there.

5

And so we arrive: here
at the house of the secret,
beneath the vaulted

stars of the sanctuary
dome, our voices made tall
by ceilings that gasped,

walls that coiled at the rim
like giant scrolls of water
inhaled out of the seas.

Such was the rapture
he conjured, having washed
at such an altar, its glass rose

a single mighty eye ahead.
Unthinkable, he thought,
the heft of caution in this,

our hospice. Irresistible,
the quiet in the shudder
of the psalm and prelude.

Go. Sleep.
Bewilder what you calm.
The sound of rain goes

where the rain cannot.

6

His instinct of the holy was never
the chosen and so not holy enough.
His instinct of the more holy

was how he walked gently like a fly
on a pool of fresh rain. His instinct
of the secret was how childhood saw

the great unflinching eye that notes
all things, the name that would hold fast
the river, the river that holds the gaze

of names. Which is to say he needed
a greater vantage point than any
man or name. He needed a Lord

the way a body needs a brain,
the way some of us need to see the King
as what he rules. Long live the King.

A child rules a world of toys.
She does not know where she ends,
the toys begin. Of those who watch,

who, if any, she will survive.

7

For those who made the journey,
a relic held the forever fading
breath of the secret, not the body

entire but the broken parts
that would one day be a body
in kind: the tooth of our Lord,

a psalm of hair, the foreskin
that brought a saint to tears,
the many foreskins of, praise God,

a single saint—each sacrament more
radiant beneath the touch.
He understood that touch,

the sacrifice that blazed
the paths of pilgrims,
the unforgiving paths that bent

their backs. Not to lose
the secrecy, but to give it
the ghost of some possession,

to give our own flesh that ghost,
that gift of the passage
from the near to the far,

to the nearness of the far.
But that was long ago. The paradise
of relics is a relic now.

Some were lost among the catacombs.
Others torched as fakes.
As if a secret died

in each, or if not died
then burned a bit, knelt down
at the shadow of the shroud

and ate.

8

But what about the flood.
Pestilence, answers the world,
a baptism of disease.

And so the secret threw
flowers like specks of blood.
There, it said, *what secret would be less*

than its creation.

9

And then a conflagration spread across
the face of a holy land
which was the cradle of secrets,

entire desert minefields of secrets;
which took the multitudes
for the few, the few for the many;

where the spirit of revenge was rage
against time—take it back:
these words made of sticks and cinders,

of the near at hand, iconography
scratched on prison walls.
Take back the wailing wall of paradise.

The star-spit of the rifle and fuse,
the cavernous bunker thumped
and smoking, brimming with ink—take that.

Take the secret few the sun takes down
like rain, like rust, like a deposition.
Or the sacred ground that opens

its mouth and nothing comes.
Gather up the slow fuel of the multitudes
smeared in oil, entire desert

minefields of oil. Wash them,
name them, carry them off.
Bear them up through the story

you hand your children
like a gun, like all the world
dragged through needle of heaven,

and see what you have left.

10

The night the secret died he was out
walking the woods, their leafy shadows
eclipsing the stars, and the trees

which long had been the legs of the sky
were no longer legs, and the stones
sealed up their boxes of jewels,

and that flinching in the branches,
the first scant sparks of rain descending,
had nothing to do with fire and angels,

being no more, he thought, than *rain*,
though even this as he said it, the word
with its arms full of leaves, waking,

was just another sound among many,
just another wind to wander overhead,
desireless among its kind,

without a place to kneel or suffer.

11
    for Stephen Crane

One life, one life, and so the multitudes
return. A secret dies in each
and so returns.

He considered the courage of living
without the secret,
how, for all he knows,

a secret admires that way of being
friends, of opening the palms
of prayer like a boat

exposed to heavy water.
There are days when heaven falls
silent, when the secrecy

does away with the secret.
Always more flowers
in the field than hands

to hold them. Some lie
on the beds of the multitudes.
They are the rivers of the field

ever losing the thing
that bears their name.
They are the small wind

that waves the fallen colors of the many,
the sun-drenched river
of the near to the far,

the joys of the field above our names
ever becoming something
corruptible, nameless, something

else. Praise them.

from *The Other Sky*
(2015)

The Delta

If you are going there by foot, prepare
to get wet. You are not you anymore.

You are a girl standing in a pool
of clouds as they catch fire in the distance.

There are laws of heaven and those of place
and those who see the sky in the water,

angels in ashes that are the delta's now.
They say if you sweep the trash from your house

after dark, you sweep away your luck.
If you are going by foot, bring a stick,

a third leg, and honor the great disorder,
the great broom of waterfowl and songbirds.

Prepare to voodoo your way, best you can,
knowing there is a little water in things

you take for granted, a little charity
and squalor for the smallest forms of life.

Voodoo was always mostly charity.
People forget. If you shake a tablecloth

outside at night, someone in your family
dies. There are laws we make thinking

it was us who made them. We are not us.
We are a floodplain by the Mississippi

that once poured slaves upriver to the fields.
We are a hurricane in the making.

We could use a magus who knows something
about suffering, who knows a delta's needs.

We understand if you want a widow
to stay single, cut up her husband's shoes.

He is not himself anyway and walks
barefoot across a landscape that has no north.

Only a ghost tree here and there, a frog,
a cricket, a bird. And if the fates are kind,

a girl with a stick, who is more at home,
being homeless, than you will ever be.

Flowerbed

To see the woman lie in a wide-eyed field
of flowers, her lids a heavy shade of blue,

her hair in fiery eddies against the leaves,
I wonder, is this look of someone half-blind

with weariness and pollen, the sweet smoke
of everything about her bursting into bloom.

Does she gaze into the distance to see
the land dissolve where the sea-fog meets it,

where all she knows trails off into the pleasure
of knowing it once and letting it fall away.

Is the glass of what she looks through glazed
in Vaseline, amazed beyond amazement,

or does she read some microscopic script
etched across the surface of the lens.

What does she know of the force that pulls her
toward a sleep she does not enter, not yet,

this earth just strange enough to be the thing
she gives her self, the chest she lies against,

sinking like a sigh. What could be better,
say the lotus eaters in their island grasses,

the diet of flowers they crush as they roll
into each other and close their eyes again.

Some sleep it off. Some long to lie down
where they are lying, already and again,

the tiny cameras of the blossoms, flashing.
Too soon the end that's late to everything.

What is it about getting home that is so
crucial now, as was the urge to leave it,

to step into some crowded train car
where faces lean into the morning paper.

Too soon the mist that veils the eye, the eye
that sets a veil on fire. Too soon the sun,

its call to something, someone in the fog,
to strike the sea with his long deep oars.

Runoff

The door to the otherworld is the mouth
of a drainpipe with a little wind inside it.

What girl could resist, her hair blown back
with the gentle force of all that darkness

as if in perfect stillness where she stands
alone and listens, she were falling through.

The door is not a door. It is a yawn
so monstrous it would swallow us whole.

It makes her smaller, more breakable
her glass heart, her jar of silent fireflies.

This is what it is to lie in the center
of some black mandala, never knowing

what source trickles through, what it is
in the shallow water between her legs,

in the body's quiet questionings,
that frees the ghost to wander off ahead.

How is it the space of sleep is larger
than the body it's in. How is it, we ask,

and the earth responds in whatever
language we would give it. It knows them all.

It understands none. Whatever water
comes this far, it comes from somewhere,

we trust. It tells us. We hear it crackle
like a million tiny typewriters.

It is writing a million tiny letters
to the part of us that writes. Or longs to.

After all we were born of it, this shadow.
So far behind we are walking toward it.

Hell. You look at anything this long,
and you are not looking anymore.

You are a girl before the unlit mirror,
who slips through, not far, but far enough.

You are the voice that oracles the tunnel,
the one you hear in the faint exchange,

when you swear there is no one, just you,
your face turned away from your face, you

the million tiny needles of the dark.
You the breeze that presses as it pulls.

The City

Let us say you are. You are the girl
who, looking out her window to the city,

takes on the gray pallor of the day,
the way some lizards take on the green

shade of the season they are in, so close
to the garden the garden cannot find them.

The cold hand reflected in the glass,
the one that touches her hand, or rather

the chill of skies that fall between them,
it mirrors a need in her, sweet with rain,

with the dark of cinderblock apartments
that just might be reaching out in turn.

They just might surprise the mirror to life
like a visitor's kiss at a prison window.

Not that the rain cares about its kisses,
or the note of sadness we bring to it.

Still the empty gleam of public benches
strangely comforts her, like superstition,

or the man who walks from last night's dream
to sit and crackle open a sheet of news.

Every page he turns is the sound of rain.
Every world a world on fire. To live in

the city is to feel it, read it, wonder
where the storm sweeps the indigents

whose eyes we once avoided in our haste.
Days like this were made to pry us open,

to dust the lonely glass of the cabinet.
Made to listen. To her, to the bare room

behind her, to the faint sound of things
as they break into small and smaller things.

This is the logic of rain, of the widow
transfixed before some beautiful reminder:

when a world goes missing, it starts to speak.
I want to know. Is there no such thing

as the whole picture until it shatters,
until it becomes a girl by a window,

a scattering of daylight tinged with night.
How much of seeing is the need to see,

and how much of needing can be seen,
crumpled in flames beneath the visible.

Is the face she looks through her face
or hers returning after an all-night trip,

its hair drenched, the sense of its body
moving still. She too longs to arrive,

to lay her silence in an open question,
a grave that loses its outline to the grass.

Or to lead to a better question, a closer
face that blurs in the drizzle of being

near, that touches her, for real this time,
and so, like water, vanishes from view.

Victor

I choose the blind eye—who can resist—
radiant as a glass of milk. I choose

to look because I cannot look away,
because it is the one lantern burning

at this hour, in this version of a boy
whose solitude is the hall I walk,

my footsteps close behind me. The good eye knows.
It takes the dark to let the darkness in.

If you are looking for that boy, look there.
Dip into the ink that bears his name.

There's a bed inside where a boy turns,
asleep, where he imagines someone like you.

But if you look without understanding
what you look for, you just might return

to the ghost eye floating in its socket,
dead to the boy, and so alive to us.

I choose the ghost because it chooses me.
For it is never knowing what goes on

and on that makes it an invitation
to the dream we cannot bring ourselves

to dream. Imagine what it is to live
with half the world swallowed in the fog.

It is nothing like that. It is nothing.
Like the place you came from you can't remember.

It's closer than we know, the little death
that opens up room for the moment, for us.

Once there was a boy named Victor who lived
in half his body. And when he looked at me,

I too was cut in half. And when he didn't,
he took from me the child he could not see.

Thomas

Not long ago he could crawl inside
a jar like this, monstrous for a jar,

tiny for the child who breathes there,
just to experiment, to be the thing

that fills the blank like a signature,
a choice. Not long ago he had no choice.

Only a womb. And in it a growth force
people take for will, but it is not,

any more than wombs are paradise.
Though they might be, in retrospect,

as knowledge is, as knowledge longs to be.
No. To fill the vacancy wherever—

in your arms, your body, another's body—
it is not heaven. Only a miracle space

where bodies begin, before they look up
to find their mothers missing from the room.

The boy who carries the jar in his arms
is missing an explanation. What is a jar

that giant for, if not for smaller boys
and the thrill of panic that they find there.

When he was smaller he asked his mother,
what is death. And his mother replied,

nothing really, nothing to worry about.
Which made it sound like a place inside her,

a place of worry, sure, but also a jar,
an emptiness like the longing that brings

a boy into the world. He came from nothing.
Not all that bad, so far as he remembers.

Like some strange thing that is about to happen.
The name we are about to be given,

the voice in the air that becomes our reason
to respond. Let us call him Thomas,

this boy with his enigma, and the jar
a specimen jar. And what he longs to study,

everything. Let us begin with that.
And what he pours into the free space

will be a little more his for being there,
his nothing a little less nothing, less free.

A collector of jars, not because he loves
any one in particular, but searching

makes him able to love, to pour his want,
his blood, from jar to jar and back again.

Such is the rhythm of a boy who walks.
When he was smaller, he asked his mother,

where did I come from. And his mother froze
a moment, hearing in her mind the word

me, and then the word *God,* and then
no word at all, which was another word

that gathered more and more significance
in time. Like sand into the hourglass.

Sea of Trees

Silence is half the music. The song breathes.
Winter chimes go still inside the trees.

And the hole in the music is musical,
because, oddly, it lets in what music

is not. Not alone. The stray cough,
the closing door. Silence is one half

merciful, the other the careless snowfall
of the world. I do not feel what you feel.

I cannot sing my way into your child's
suffering. I try. And the music of trying

goes speechless in the woods between us.
Let me try again. Once there was a girl

who climbed a tree to end her misery,
to hang among the branches like a bell.

Pain is pain. It is not beautiful.
What we do not know about her life

fills the forest with a light blue mist.
So why look, you ask. Is it her there.

Or is it your heartbreak that is a shade
cruel, not knowing what it is you break for.

Pain is not the music of pain. Not love.
Though it may find comfort in the light

blue distance, I know from experience,
this is not always true. Nerves go raw.

Too raw for the quietest of breezes.
Would it have mattered if the song were sad,

if it were less the theater of sadness.
The sandal that slipped her dangling foot,

its needle of endearment, does it charm,
does it paralyze love's will a little.

Half a girl in pain is our deafness to pain.
Unlike the deafness of the trees in winter,

we pretend. We try. We commit
our gaffes at the funeral reception,

and the mother crumples into tears.
It is our innocence that makes mistakes,

that makes us feel more cautious and ashamed.
Is it better to look or not look.

Or to desecrate the season. True.
In turning away, we turn into something.

What would comfort a lost innocent more.
Or is that the question. Is it not

the mother we should worry about now.
Is it not the blue gem of love she offered.

Is it not the sweet song she sang her child,
to make night safe for sleeping, once again.

New Poems

The Invention of the Radio Telescope

When Karl Jansky put an ear to the sky,
he discovered three things: near storms,

far storms, and a hiss of unknown origin.
The unseen, as we know it, has a body.

You hear it crackle in the star fire.
When I was a kid I prayed for as much,

moved the radio needle slowly through
the fields of nowhere looking for a voice.

Some forms of panic are so shy, so quiet,
they nearly disappear. They have no face

and so wear the eyes a fear would give them.
Fear of something, anything, please.

I know this because I had a mother
who collected boxes, jeweled, carved, sealed

with keys too small to find us. Each click
entombed the little nothing that she put there.

I am told there is no such thing as silence
since there will always be a hum of nerves.

Or is it stars. How could we possibly tell.
Karl Jansky, you understand what it is

to stay up all night unsure of what you hear.
The instruments of heaven will tell you,

nothing fits in no box. It presses an ear
to the heart that says, here I am, no, here, here.

Keats

1

Say you lie in your convalescence
by a cold window latched at the crossbeam,

and the heads of roses have turned brown
and heavy on their stems, so you stare

through a lens of words that would preserve them,
preserve even this sensation of you here

kneeling, leaning to the book below.
You stare until, it seems, the words are rose,

your eyes the chameleon turned the color
of earth, your skin turned the glass gone cold.

It connects you the way windows connect
and shield. And something unseen in the weather

enters, something in acquiescence of rain
that falls right through the silence of the room.

2

And if you lie long enough and still,
you begin to talk to things as things

talk back. On the mantelpiece, an urn,
its mouth full of ashes, its lone cow

glazed into the clay, roped, compliant,
lowing in the meadow that leads downhill.

And you too are entering that town
at the end of a journey, that citadel

abandoned to the elements, and still
you piece yourself together there, in steeple

tunes sounded out in silent mourning
that needs you, hears you, hears itself

in those you lost and have no words for,
hymns that fail the spell of their occasion.

3

Say you stare hard and cold at one small thing,
so long, in time, it longs to take your place,

to change your angels into men, men
to women, the ruminations of your skin

to dust you sweep not knowing it is yours.
Say you hear in it the moan of those led

to slaughter, echoes that are one part beast,
the other emptiness, the other a jar

of wine before an emptiness has filled it.
Say the bottle you drink says something

foolish, like: *if you cannot be wise,
be a mystery.* Do not judge too harshly.

Or curse beyond all better judgment the power
of things to make us hopeful and confused.

4

Do not silence this thing that suffers us,
carries us, turns us into windows

and beasts and the breathing machinery
clouds rumble halfway down the mountain.

Wine turns to blood one way or another
as all things seen, written, seen again

in convalescence, when our bodies turn
back to flesh. When the bottle talks,

it does so with a measure of compassion,
as in *com,* and *passion,* bearing with,

as in: the roses bear with us our fire,
or a drunkard's death his emptiness.

O attic dust, said the bottle he lay
inside. *Whose mouth is not a jar of ashes.*

5

We love who we love, says the rock star
who goes from beauty to beauty breaking vows.

He who is untrue, whose music rises
on the charts and falls like stars and starlets.

He too is beautiful. A throb, a flame,
a fist pinned against a young girl's wall

to beat against the obstacle and break it.
Just what the heart would enter with its noise

is noise. Perfect silence is never ours
though we sense it somewhere. Beneath the ink

of the retirement contract, the white we lie in.
We love who we love, says the bottle

to a friend, and the words make a circle.
And a circle a mirror. Waiting for a face.

6

Long ago the word *true* meant undying,
as arrows were when the eye looked down

the arrow in the eye. But that was then,
before we pulled the arrow out in tears.

The word *true* meant the passing moan
of ships in fog was a shadow, and shadows

a fall from some enduring shade of black.
And the consolation was real enough

and so it did not last. I have a friend
whose husband left behind a radio

that plays in a far corner of the house.
And sure, the music came from somewhere, else.

But what does it care. No matter the source
of real grief that has no music in it.

7

The foster children of our silence say,
if you cannot solve a problem, smother it

in bronze. Or is it music. Sometimes we know
we are wrong for each other—the world

and I—and so, together, wrong the world
as we know it. We love who we love,

not for who they are but what they leave
behind in the corner of our house.

If I say the unheard tunes are sweeter,
call it the belladonna of saying things

true and untrue, to cut the flesh in two.
Who would not diversify our futures

to lessen the blow. Or leave a radio
in the distance, with no one there to hear it.

8

This is not a prayer, says the urn in prayer.
It is a woman kneeling in the churchyard

to read the name of someone she used to know.
This voice that blossoms from the artifact,

it speaks with all the fire of a church
that slowly turns to nails. The urn knows:

the cow in the meadow deserves a voice.
Not his of course. That vanished long ago.

The forever pictured who goes to slaughter,
he deserves to be heard the way silence

never is. And yet we have the word for it.
We have an urn whose waist shaped the hand

that gave it shape and fire and, in time, real
wine once. And women looking up to drink.

9

Bells of grief and marriage are one bell now,
and unheard music nothing without music.

Like an emptiness without a vessel.
Or the widows of experience in homes.

If urns could simply speak or not, the steeples
of these flowers would stumble to their knees.

Pure madness has no wonder, pure water
no obstacle, no world. I am asking you,

do not judge too harshly. You the child
of your childhood. The silent bride

who wanders from the others through the woods
at dusk. And if you come upon a clearing,

you pause. You listen. In your still white gown,
your body trembling. Expectant as a bell.

The Interiors

> When a man is in despair, it means that he still believes in something.
> —DMITRI SHOSTAKOVICH

Another hour, another steeple of bells,
and St. Petersburg is listening to its ghost

bronze fall into the porticos in hiding,
into Dmitri where he leans across the keys

to carve his initials in a string quartet;
a gesture that says, if you are listening,

you are listening to me, among the winter
lilacs, the sleepers in their walls of music,

the music in the tyrant who cannot sleep.
I have held so much back, so long, so deep,

I sign my name *no country but this.* This toll
that names no one and so. A little of each.

Each night I am waiting with my suitcase
by my bed, listening for a knock to take me,

make me. I am watching my patriots vanish
without trace. Or none but this. These bells

whose gravity bends my head to the staves.
These flowers that read by their own soft light.

Blackout Starlight

At the base of a leg
of smoke

    on which the heaven of Los Angeles
    stands, a man

is burning
the unidentified remains

    of a chair
    in a can, and his shadow

grows tall
against the warehouse wall

    behind his eyes.
    Another man joins him,

and in the distance you
hear a siren,

    a dog,
    and then another,

and the whispered sea of the interstate
coming ashore.

    In other words
    a kinship of silhouettes

and voices
falls over the talk and inner lives

    of those who otherwise might appear
    left out

of the larger conversation.
I read once

    fire came to the center
    of our social circle

for this: before it cooked our meats
it held

    our fascination. It held us.
    And then the howling,

and a man shares a hit
of smoke

    with a man swept
    with the others from the center

of town.
The new money is buying

    up the old
    and the rents that sweep

beds from these apartments,
and the mission

    is full,
    and the flames keep breaking

some local ordinance
to pieces

    like a chair.
    Just today the one man sat

through a sermon
in a parking lot

    because it came with coffee
    and a roll

and a city of angels
that had no suffering.

    Only strangers
    to their experience

on earth.
It felt like a story told

    over the fire.
    The stars taking aim

among the copters with their needles
of light.

    Something in the sermon's voice rose
    with a clarity

foreign to smoke.
It helps some. The coffee

    is hot.
    And the new money keeps burning

a hole in the pockets
of Los Angeles

    where land is cheap and people
    move along

a step ahead of the law and the seasons.
Welcome to paradise,

    says the postcard of a beach
    in the fire.

And as it crumples, nothing
changes.

    Nothing moves an address
    like that,

where the streets are swept each morning
by machine.

    There is a better world,
    surely,

and the darkness of the warehouse wall
ebbs a little

    as the ashes rise.
    Whatever the medication, it is always

wearing off.
Whatever the angel

    dust that falls from the construction,
    power is always

hungry, thin,
gone the way of white powders

    in the high rise
    and the air above the earth movers

coming to rest.
Any pretense here of the whole

    picture
    gives way to the perspective

of a man or two.
Beside the empty warehouse,

    words and silences get exchanged
    like cash

buying cash,
and the larger conversation

    is less a conversation
    then the ghost of elsewhere

thumping in a black
limousine,

    the windows the mirror of our own
    exclusion.

One's own hand could be shaking
for some

    unspoken reason.
    One man could hear the siren spread,

dog to dog, and laugh
with another,

    and what the hell.
    Time to put the whole enchilada

in,
the chair and the missing man

>   it held,
>   the leg with its claw,

the arm
curved like a broken overpass.

>   Time
>   for the part that never was a chair.

It is now.
Fire makes it so

>   and so mails the postcard back
>   to where it came from,

to St. Peter
at the electric gate,

>   beyond the local ordinance that is the space
>   around a heaven,

that keeps it safe.
Put it in,

>   the angel and the machine and the ball
>   that drops

through the wall of the tenement,
the bright flock

>   that scatters like a window.
>   Put them all in,

the way a dog puts it all
in the cry

    we call his,
    though something the size of the whole

picture
is happening to him,

    —echo untouched by echo,
    throat by throat—

something of the whole heart
cut out

    of hiding, the deep red part
    hurled into the dark

like meat
to the wall,

    and the shadows roar.

Bone

1

Then my hound laid his head on my leg
and sighed, *You know, bones are overrated.*

I know, I said. *Sad shadow of a meal,
that scent of meat a torment really, a ghost*

*of better things better left alone.
Do you want one?* And his tail said yes,

dogged by a lust for blood and fat
and the promise of a better world

inside the bone, of a body's final will
and testament inside the residual vault.

He would eat pure hunger if I had some,
and the crackle of the jaw would speak

the words of boots and gravel, and the road,
as hunger promised it, would never end.

2

That is why I have a dog. And bones
to give away. Pauses in conversation

hilarious with the beasty crumpling.
Because I need a better way to say,

we are only human. I need a yard
full of sticks and lilies to remind me

this plot is mine in name only, this name
a gift I give away. We go way back,

my pooch and I, and he knows I know
he thinks he knows me, when in fact

he does, and lo, a bone. Which is not mine
to give exactly, but that is how it is

with currency changing hands, hands
changing structure. It started with a bone.

3

My father told me, there really *is* flesh in there,
embedded in the bone's matrix of salt.

There is, if you work it, energy to burn.
And after that, more bone, more flesh, more work.

Bodies are overrated, he said, and so
he chose fire in the end. It surprised me,

the weight of ash. Much of which was salt.
Here, you carry them, said my brother,

and I imagined a certain substance inside,
without form, save the one we gave it,

like the scent of lilies we name a *lily*
and lay on the iron sands of the garden.

There really *is* bone there, I thought, in bronzes
and the bronze tones of those who kneel to read them.

4

I call my dog, among the other things,
dog. It was his name before him,

and will be when we are long forgotten.
Which you is you anyway, I ask him,

and he acts a little here-nor-there.
When it comes to specifics, it's the voice

he likes, the give and take of it, the music.
There is no free lunch, my father said

when I was small, and then he fed me.
Imagine if words were not approximations.

Who would answer them. Who would exhume
the you that hides, locked in you, like bone.

Who would claim it. Come, I say, when I
am lost. Come, sweet dog. And then he comes.

5

Is it any wonder the world's on fire
with the vanitas portraits of skulls

and candles whose still and priceless light
belies them. All is vanity, they say,

and here we are, at a small museum
in the heart of a town whose name escapes me.

Each day I leap from my bones a little,
the way light leaps from a painted candle

into darkness, or a dog into the woods.
A skull is a lantern in a place like this.

When I think of the bones of the hand,
I see the puzzle it takes a painter to solve.

I see white, though I know they must be
black in there, so long as they are painting.

6

If you weigh a body before and after
its final breath, you are probably not

a member of the family. It gets lighter,
as if the missing life had volume, weight.

The lords of gravity are in us, and still
we know so little about them. My dog says,

A part of a thing cannot cause that thing,
and I look back at him in disbelief.

To think each cause must first touch a shadow
between things, between *things* with shadows

and those with none. Hunger touches jaw
touches bone touches those who turn to dogs

for solace. Long after the deer that leapt
from earth: bone that keeps leaping from the bone.

7

Here by the fire and crackle of our jaws,
I take comfort knowing companionship

begins in unanswered questions. Here,
side by side, in light of the open freezer.

Good dog, I say, when he excels at being
that, a dog, like a child before she knows

she is. *Good dog,* I hear my mother say,
now that she is gone, beyond the voice

of her own mother, but never the desire.
Good dog, says mother before mother

in an endless howl of mothers to the sea.
Bone fights bone to remain just that.

To make it what it is, hard, good in ways
hunger knows, before the jaw destroys it.

8

My dog takes his chisel to the thing
he carves the goodness from. Like a sculptor

who takes from rock the part that makes it
memorial. To make of loss an art,

imagine the space around the fullness,
and you are closer to the life lived and so

destroyed. I do not ask this of a dog:
seeing what he does not. If he is good,

the seeing dog is lantern to the blind,
those who trace with hands wings of the marble.

To see as sculptors see begins in blindness.
To hunger like a dog. Now and then bones

appear on graves, but mostly it is angels.
I do not ask for meat from an angel.

9

The angelic made of bone will tell you,
Angels are overrated. That is their calling,

to be the mother's face above the cradle
long after the mother is gone. Tonight

the dogs of my neighbors lift their howls
into one music made of lonely hours.

A woman takes on the pallor of her sheets.
In time, as I remember, she disappears.

When I think of her, I am always leaving
out the essentials. I am hungry. Always.

I want to say that she is letting go
of something when she says my name in tears.

I want to say they measure me—her eyes—
my heart laid in a pan of the balance.

10

Then my hound laid his head on my leg
and sighed, and the words he might have said

left for the words he never could quite say.
The bone he was working over vanished

to a place in hiding, where earth was fresh.
Doubtless the sorry shape of bone changed

in ways a dog remains the better judge.
Still bones will be bones. I imagine.

Our common grave is lit by the lonely
flashlight of those who lay their weight on ours.

The parts we tore away are turning into
blood. *Good dog,* I whisper, as if to say

good night to night. No. To all nights now.
And then the slow unearthing of the stars.

New Moon

Then my teacher told me to close my eyes
and observe the observer of the observer

and so on, down the long path of seeing,
the chiaroscuro of thought in the distance

like a field of starlight when the power goes.
See the seer, she said, and as I breathed

in waves against the dark, I saw my teacher.
I saw her porch lit with prayer flags

from Tibet: a light wind in the word *flag*,
a lighter word in the wind departing.

How it all fit in there, I will never know:
the flags, the words, the black canvas starred

in needles. And her, or my idea of her,
descending the stairs on her mechanical

chair devised for those who suffer daily
steps and thresholds beyond my understanding.

She told me once, you hear a note of suffering
in the higher resonance of laughter.

I confess. I do not hear the better half
of what I hear, though I feel the pull there

of missing things, of earth and its burden
beneath the pale lamentation of waves.

She is gone now. And shows up every time
I see a chair like this. I hear her curse

her feet of stone, not knowing I am there.
God, she says softly to herself.

They say the new moon can be traced in
the faint deflected sunrays of the planet.

That the sky we see is always bigger
than how we see it. Stars and mirrors.

Stars and dead stars. Tell me, teacher
in your field on fire. What else is there.

The Sculpture Garden

1. Eve (Auguste Rodin)

Those were days the sky held the earth
in its blood-rinsed linen, and the words

she spoke were so much weather in the garden,
so much memory that cannot see the one

who remembers, only, at best, a ghost:
the wind in the flute of the lung, the rib,

the couple and the holes where music goes.
Every garden needs a hole somewhere,

and every hole the wall to give it shelter,
snakes who slither from their skins, refreshed.

We all do it: leave body after body,
and what we forget is the white space

on which we write the memoirs of our youth:
regret that is the past tense of desire.

Take this Eve crumpled beneath the shame
that is not hers alone but an animus

she carries as a flute carries a tune
or chins the blood of the hand that struck them.

If you look at an apple long enough,
it begins to dream of sweetness and teeth,

to ripen into the blush you see there.
This is a story after all and so seen

with eyes that pour the black light of the mind
over all things given, gardened, made.

There are just so many arms to conceal
one's nakedness, to embrace one's self

which is another word for no one now,
which is another word for leaving home.

Bite into this fruit and you begin
to tell a story. And you begin to give

your burden of unruliness and want
to others if only to see them, curse them,

take them back into your arms knowing
something of your cruel truth. It takes years

of crumpling in your own fire to see it.
Eve is lovely still. As is her suffering.

The love you know knows both now. It must.
It will. And you are learning to bear that,

your beauty fading. And you are breaking what
you know into a thousand lovely pieces.

2. Hammering Man (Jonathan Borofsky)

The hammer that made the very first hammer
was a man made of nails who so loved

the world he hit hard until it sparked.
Kids know: the floor is hostile and so we learn

to walk it, love it, pound our first music
through, to rely on the impersonal

as bodies rely on bones they never meet
in person. A certain holding back gives

the nail a place in congress to seat its power:
waves glide into the oiled slip, lovers

into roads thatched in vines and alders
until there is no road, and headlights darken.

The road that led to the very first road
knows what it is to love the riot and structure

of virgin woods and music from the dash,
to enter heaven the way a thread enters

the eye it blinds. Needles know: it takes
a little wounding of the cloth to mend it.

I wounded my very first because I was
her first, slow as I unhooked the steel

button in her jeans and so broke
the circle, my hands all eyes and blind.

I did not know then what I was making
when I was made, how the pool I entered

concealed a vague sensation of return.
And it was the newness that brought us

back and ghosted all things half-remembered.
Look at him, the hammering man, head

bowed like the steel he holds as if they prayed
to the same god. No, there is no idol

here, for, in striking back, the world is
an instrument of some larger power

of surprise. The fiercest iron is a hall
with a door at the end we never reach.

It could be our door, the one on the porch
with a rip in the screen that whistled. It could

lead to a better life. And therefore does.
Our very first door, banging in the wind.

3. Quantum Cloud (Antony Gormley)

If a man were made of wind, he would need
a coat to rustle, a cloud of leaves to slip through.

Otherwise who is he. Whose coat is whose.
He would need shoes with laces in a frenzy

flagging down the hands that tried to tie them.
Every bite would startle from its fork,

every word from his papers, every promise.
I know this man. Some days he has no skin

other than the world and what it touches,
as if love killed itself to become stronger.

Some days he verges on a break through.
Or break down. Who, asks the quickened breath.

Who, the eye in the ring of the eye below.
The needles of excitement are close to dread.

I know this woman. She has a dry wound
that will not close, a door without a tongue.

What is closer at heart than estrangement
and the many paths home: the hammer, the lover,

the flame. The needles of excitement thread
the pores with air. You have a choice there,

among the nightmares that tell you, softly,
you are not alone. If a woman were made

of wind, she would be searching our pockets
for what she lost. The physiology

of dread is close to arousal. Some days
it seems a lie, the sense of displacement

and theft, of breaking and entering. I know
this woman who wore the shadow I laid there.

And together we were a tornado of pins.
And together our shadow darkened as it cried.

4. Bronze Crowd (Magdalena Abakanowicz)

More than one way to die into life,
more than one you that dies. I got lost once,

looking at the headless, and so vanished.
Then I reappeared in them, vaguely,

and vanished once again. Only now,
looking back, I see attention as longing

to be given. And so received. Now
I see the hand inside the hole of a face.

More than one way to wear the sky
on your shoulders, to be part of something

greater. A language of a more capacious
politics has the face of politics still.

Headless men and women turn to bronze
in the garden. Bronze continues to turn.

If there is a headsman here, he too
is headless. Though who are we to know.

He keeps vanishing into his victims
whose suffering is power. Theirs. His.

Pick your poison. Each body stands
weathered just so: to be the suffering

of one. No two the same. And so they suffer
these hours in the garden, being none.

A heart breaks for any one. But shatters
for all. *All* that is a word of bronze.

Once, in the garden, there was no crowd.
My father had the face of the only

soldier I knew. He told me nothing
of his suffering, a little of his creed.

I have a picture of his ship eroding
into ocean fog. I love that picture.

I ask it: does one seaman kneel
to an ocean so singular inside you,

he goes speechless; do terms of a new
creed begin in there, where they end.

Hard to think in a place like that.
To be mindful, useful. Find the words.

Hard to say your death is yours alone.
Isn't that your dying. Might ours be

one gray day in Whittier, California.
The unfolding of the black umbrellas,

a sudden flock of crows. Bear with me.
More than one way to die into life.

The ash-box wrapped in a birthing blanket.
The mainsail swallowed in the fog of all.

5. Night (Aristide Maillol)

Who are we to judge, her skin stripped
to the black bronze now, arms crossed, head bowed,

weary as the eyes of flowers that darken
as they curl. Turn a portrait to the wall.

It just might see, in time, what she sees:
the hall of shadow that is neither wall

nor portrait, but both, as blazes are
both the wood and what the woods become.

A statue too is never still, but a hall
that leads from room to room. Hand to eye,

eye to star, sculptor to the handwork he
continues, late, when France has gone to sleep.

I was driving on a stretch of highway
in Kansas once and killed the headlight,

and as my heartbeat sped into the dark,
I thought it was the future. I thought I would

keep driving long after I lay down to dream.
I looked at a girl and saw my future

in hers, disappointed at dawn, like stars.
This garden is full of bodies that are hers,

eyes that plow the fields they read, they harvest,
shadows laid down in a snow of shadows.

A statue made of shadows is one part flower,
the other a hub in the wheel of leaves.

Who are we to be apart from each,
our face pressed before us like a shield.

If a statue holds the posture of evening,
do not say she turns her back on day.

She does. But a girl lived there once.
In the shape of some loss or disappointment.

A girl filled that space with blood no longer
there. The sculpture garden is closing soon.

And one by one the guard snaps the trances
of those slow to notice. One by one

statues turn their backs to break the sunlight
open. To give, as one, each face away.

Furrow

And I walked until I came to a field
the color of paper, and in that field

was every other color and the things
in colored fields they came from. Thus:

the desire that has no shade but takes
on the shadow of everything it longs

to include, as if this were the way
out of a point of view. But into what

was the question that was never
everything. A field a field of vision

after all and so approached as the rustle
of crows in the corn must be to be

there. And what was missing was one
man I know whose particular face—

engrossed, furrowed as a good book
over breakfast—longs to be just that:

his look alone, and so quite possibly
companioned. Less the mirror of some

imagined harvest. More the coordinate
of the ordinary, the chosen, the loved.

The summons of the face made
sharp and personal the alternative

to one I never see. Is that you, it asked,
you the beleaguered taken as one.

And I had to set apart the great
cornfield to see him against it, as one

longs to see a shadow wander off, alone,
or the writer in the voice that says, dear reader.

I wanted to hear one man speak a tongue
we shared and did not quite, for he

had difficulty with the edges of words
and startled at a cry in the field. First terror,

then crows, then one among the many, the once
unnamed and so invisible, then named,

relished, and then unnamed in order to be
seen. Once more the horizons of corn, the dark

crackle approaching—where are you, dear
father, my namesake and disappearance,

and why here, now, and late at that, why
the porch with its crow-hinge that shrieks behind you,

not you but some damaged version of you
I must walk through. Into the fields you loved.

www.ingramcontent.com/pod-product-compliance
Lightning Source LLC
Chambersburg PA
CBHW020813230426
43666CB00007B/992